This book should b[...]   [...] of the
Lancashire County   date

D0714651

RESOLVE YOUR DIFFERENCES

Seven steps to coping with
conflict in your relationship

ANDREW G. MARSHALL

BLOOMSBURY
LONDON · BERLIN · NEW YORK · SYDNEY

First published in Great Britain 2011

Copyright © 2011 by Andrew G. Marshall

The moral right of the author has been asserted

Some of this material has appeared in a different context in *I Love You But I'm Not In Love With You*, published by Bloomsbury.

Bloomsbury Publishing Plc
36 Soho Square
London W1D 3QY

Bloomsbury Publishing, London, New York and Berlin

A CIP catalogue record for this book is
available from the British Library

ISBN 978 1 4088 0259 5

10 9 8 7 6 5 4 3 2 1

Typeset by Hewer Text UK Ltd, Edinburgh
Printed in Great Britain by Clays Limited, St Ives Plc

MIX
Paper from
responsible sources
FSC® C018072

www.bloomsbury.com/andrewgmarshall

Seven steps to coping with conflict in your relationship

INTRODUCTION

Seven Steps is a series of books offering straight-forward advice for creating successful and fulfilling relationships. Getting the most out of love needs skills, and the good news is that these skills can be taught. Nowhere is this more important than in resolving disputes. Time and again, the most significant breakthrough in couple counselling is when both partners can talk about their feelings and know they will be given a fair hearing.

No matter how ingrained a problem is or how many irritating little things come between you, good communication will smooth the way to a better future together.

In this book, I will help you take a fresh look at your relationship, unpick unhelpful styles of arguing, explain the rules for positive engage-ment, develop your assertiveness and learn how to post-mortem an argument so that problems are laid to rest. Throughout the book, there are exercises to try out these techniques. Don't worry if your partner is sceptical as improving *your* problem-solving skills will lower the overall tension, make it easier to communicate and, by modelling positive argument techniques, you will be encouraging your partner to change his or hers.

In devising this programme, I have drawn on twenty-five years' experience working as a marital therapist. However, I have changed names, details and sometimes merged two or three of my clients' stories to protect their identity and confidentiality.

Andrew G. Marshall
www.andrewgmarshall.com

STEP 1

TAKING STOCK

What is the best predictor of a long and happy relationship? Coming from similar backgrounds? Common interests, ambitions and attitudes? A healthy sex life? Support from family and friends? All of these are useful, but ultimately not decisive. Numerous research projects have come to the same conclusion. It doesn't matter how many problems a couple face, or how difficult they are; the best predictor for happiness is how well they are handled.

It should be reasonably easy to disagree with our partner, put our point of view across, debate the differences and find a compromise. After all, we love each other and want the best for each other. But this is just one of the many paradoxes about love. The more that we love someone, the more it hurts if they are upset and the more we hurt if they reject us. So while a dispute with a colleague or a run-in with a stranger can be shrugged off fairly easily, one with a partner is doubly painful and therefore doubly difficult to resolve.

Worse still, there are no lessons at school on how to argue effectively and make up afterwards, and if you did not learn at home (because your parents set the negative example of sulking for days or tearing into each other), it is even harder to know where to start. That's why I have designed my seven-step programme. It will help you foster attitudes that take the sting out of disagreements, recognise bad habits, put your case in an assertive but not aggressive way, listen to your partner respectfully, post-mortem a row and, ultimately, *resolve your differences*.

The first step in my programme is to take stock and understand how you and your partner settle disputes.

WHAT'S YOUR ARGUING STYLE?

This quiz puts the spotlight on your relationship's strengths and weaknesses, and provides some targeted advice:

1. Your partner leaves his or her shoes where you can trip over them, or clothes where they don't belong. What is your reaction? Do you:

a) Count to ten;
b) Think your partner is thoughtless, lazy or disrespectful;
c) Decide you really must speak to him or her?

2. Your partner needs to spend time away from home for his or her job or hobby. This leaves you looking after the kids – again. Do you:
   a) Inwardly seethe and feel taken for granted – however, complain only to your mother, a friend or not at all;
   b) Get your revenge by being uncooperative or by coming up with lots of obstacles;
   c) Agree but ask him or her to cover a night out with your friends in return?

3. What is the unofficial motto of your relationship?
   a) Don't make waves.
   b) When it's good it's very, very good and when it's bad it's horrid.
   c) Together we can take on the world.

4. Your partner has an irritating habit – like slurping tea. What do you do about it?
   a) Sigh. You've spoken about it before.
   b) Make a sarcastic comment.
   c) Ask him or her to wait until it's not so hot.

5. You make an amorous advance in bed but your partner is not in the mood and would prefer a cuddle instead. How do you react? Do you:
  a) Have a half-hearted cuddle but privately resolve not to risk rejection in the future;
  b) Turn your back and make him or her feel guilty or know how it feels to be turned down;
  c) Enjoy the cuddle but talk about it the next day and explain how upset you felt?

6. You are in the car together and you're lost, late and tired. What happens next?
  a) You sulk and finish the journey in silence.
  b) Your partner complains about your map-reading and you blame him or her for taking the wrong turning.
  c) You ask for directions.

7. Your partner arranges for his or her parents, whom you can cope with only in small doses, to visit for a long weekend without asking. Do you:
  a) Invite friends round to lessen the burden and help the weekend go smoothly;
  b) Get angry and have it out;
  c) Explain why the decision hurts and what would make it easier?

8. It's a hot summer's day and an attractive man or woman walks past wearing very little. What do you do? Do you:

   a) Pretend not to notice as it avoids a nasty row;

   b) Check your partner is not ogling them and get upset if he or she looks twice;

   c) Tease each other or point out the beautiful stranger's failings?

9. Your electricity bill is huge. What happens next?

   a) Each of you makes pointed comments over the next few days about lights left on.

   b) You accuse each other of being wasteful and bring up other bad habits.

   c) You agree on a plan for saving energy and money.

10. Which of the following do your arguments most closely resemble?

   a) An on/off switch. Either one or the other of you wants to talk or is annoyed, but seldom both at the same time.

   b) Cat and dog fight. Lots of rough and tumble with both sides losing their temper.

   c) A debating chamber. Although things can get heated, everybody gets their say.

Mostly a): Low conflict

The two of you get on well enough and life runs smoothly, but there is very little passion. Sometimes, it can seem that you are more brother and sister than husband and wife. Don't panic, it is possible to get the passion back. The first step is to admit to the problem and the second is to stop side-stepping things that irritate you or pretending that they don't matter. Contrary to popular opinion, arguing is good for your relationship. It sorts out what is truly important and creates a sense that something needs to change. Expressing anger, making up and finally sorting out a compromise is the most intimate thing a couple can do. Isn't it time you showed your partner that you care? (You will find Chapter Two particularly helpful.)

Mostly b): High conflict

There is plenty of passion in your relationship, but is it always positive? Although you are not afraid to let rip, the rows just tend to push you and your partner into separate corners rather than solve anything. When you're upset, the automatic response is to punish – either by withdrawing or criticising. Guess what? Your partner will sink down to your level and the relationship becomes trapped in a negative downward spiral. Why not lead by example and do something nice instead? Your partner might not immediately respond in kind, but before long he or she will feel better disposed and ready to return the favour. Miracle of miracles, you have set up a positive circle. It just takes somebody to make the first move. Why not you? Don't expect your partner to change overnight; in fact, he or she will probably be suspicious, but be patient. After three or four weeks, you should see a difference. With your relationship on an even keel, you are ready to discuss what went wrong. (You will find Chapter Three particularly useful.)

Mostly c): Medium conflict

You don't overreact to problems and you don't ignore them. Congratulations for finding the middle path. However, be wary, especially if you answered 'a' or 'b' to some questions, as certain topics or being tired and stressed can still overwhelm your arguing skills. Under these circumstances, the atmosphere at home can easily turn from happy into dissatisfied. Probably about 30 per cent of couples who seek my help have medium-conflict relationships. (You will find Chapter Five, 'How to Argue Effectively', particularly helpful, but please read the other chapters to understand how arguments can turn sour.)

The Paradox of Love

The more we love our partner, the more important his or her love becomes and the more frightened we are of losing it. So we worry that if we don't do what our partner wants, then he or she will reject us. Conversely, if our partner does not go along with what we want or think is for the best, we can begin to question if she or he truly loves us. It is not surprising that small things can quickly escalate and the stakes become sky-high.

So how do we deal with different tastes, standards and attitudes? Every relationship faces this problem, partly because no two people are alike, but mainly because we are programmed to choose a partner who makes up for the qualities we lack. In the best-case scenario, these differences are catalysts for growth rather than conflict.

However, difference can become so threatening that each partner will adopt strategies to either side-step the problem or take charge and get their own way. Nobody sets out to be either a doormat or controlling – they just get frightened. Here comes the paradox: almost everything we do is to protect us from pain, but most of the pain we feel comes from this protective behaviour.

Here are five major patterns that couples adopt to deal with their differences:

Control/Compliance

One partner is in charge and the other falls in with their wishes. From traditional sitcoms, we would immediately recognise the overbearing wife and the timid husband. However, in real relationships, it is often more complex, with couples swapping control and capitulating over different issues. For example, with Martin, a thirty-two-year-old lorry driver, and his partner, Angie, a twenty-eight-year-old office manager, it was Martin who was in charge of their social life. He would decide where and with whom they spent their leisure time, would hold court with their group of friends, and decide how long they stayed. Angie would go along with his wishes. However, Angie controlled almost everything in the home: the budget, where everything was kept, what they ate, when and how they washed up; and Martin would fall in with these dictates. Some couples can rub along with these tight demarcations for years, until something breaks down the walls. In the case of Martin and Angie, it was the arrival of a baby. She found herself overwhelmed at home and he found the restrictions on their social life impossible.

Control is also more complex than just ordering somebody about or physically intimidating them. Sometimes to the outside world, the half that seems the weaker is actually very controlling. Some of the techniques to take charge, without seeming to, include: angry tears, 'poor me' tears, illness, threats of leaving, guilt-inducing body language (like sighing or raised eyebrows), blame, accusations and lectures. Although this list makes control/compliance seem exhausting, in most cases the behaviour provides a superficial peaceful coexistence. However, the compliant partner will feel more relaxed and spontaneous when the controlling partner is not around. Martin felt he could truly relax at home only when Angie was not in. Meanwhile, Angie felt more herself – and certainly not watching every word for fear of upstaging Martin – on the rare occasions that she went out with her girl friends.

Indifference/Indifference

These relationships are deceptively calm, with few lows or highs. The two lives run side by side, in parallel, but the couple have given up wanting much from each other. These relationships were common in the first half of the twentieth century when the vast majority put most emphasis on survival of the marriage and considered their personal happiness less important. The modern equivalent of indifference – withdrawing both emotionally and physically – is the workaholic relationship. Here one partner might claim to want more couple time, but always has an excuse for a few more hours on the home computer. Rather than challenging this behaviour, their partner gets on with his or her life. Other distancing behaviour includes: watching television, getting drunk, sport and burying oneself in hobbies.

Generally with indifference/indifference there is little talk, no intimacy and plenty of boredom. These couples tell me: 'We have little in common but the kids.' Peter and Nancy had been married for twenty years, but Nancy complained, 'I don't feel I really know Peter, he seems withdrawn all the time.' While Peter countered, 'What's the point in talking? All we ever discuss is work and other people.' By avoiding conflict, they had never really opened up on the issues that would let them explore and understand each other. Although both 'indifference' partners will have strong separate identities, there is no couple identity. Especially after the children become less central in their lives, one half of these couples will find the loneliness unbearable. Remember, deep down nobody is truly indifferent. Someone might pretend, or give the appearance of not caring. However, everybody wants to be loved.

Compliance/Compliance

These are the relationships where both partners are so keen to make each other happy that they give up their individuality for a couple identity. Kate and David not only worked for the same company but also sat beside each other in the staff canteen at lunchtime. When I asked if they ever thought of sitting with their individual work colleagues for a change, they both admitted being bored with the current arrangement. 'It would be nice to chat with other people,' said Kate, 'and then I'd have something to tell David in the evening.' David put it slightly differently but came to the same conclusions. So why hadn't he said anything? 'I thought it was what Kate wanted,' he explained.

Compliance might seem like the best way to run a relationship; after all, the ability to compromise is essential for a happy partnership. But these couples are so frightened of difference, and therefore so defensive, that they ignore any painful feelings. In other relationships the pain would turn to anger and a row. If Kate and David had argued, one of them would have blurted out: 'Don't crowd in on me at lunchtime.'

Control/Control

Each half of the couple wants to change the other and even small issues become a power struggle. There are lots of threats and name-calling and ugly opinions pour out in the middle of an argument. Each partner believes that if only the other followed their path, everything in the garden would be rosy. When one or other partner is winning, he or she feels powerful and vindicated, but the other partner knows all their weak spots and it is not long before the roles are reversed.

Christina and Fabio had an explosive relationship. It had started as a passionate affair but day-to-day living – when their differences could no longer be ignored – became impossible. In counselling, they spent a whole session fighting about the best way to stack a dishwasher. When I asked what the argument was really about, Fabio replied: 'She wants to control me.' He had hardly finished the sentence before Christina leapt in:

'What about you? You get upset if I wear anything even remotely sexy. I feel like a teenager having to pass a clothes check before I go out.' They were immediately into another round of fighting.

Although the periods when these couples kiss and makeup provide a high, the periods when they are fighting are a terrible low. For this reason, control/control couples are forever splitting up and getting back together again – sometimes for years on end. It seems they can't live together but can't live without each other. To break this cycle, each partner has to understand the source of their anger, show their vulnerability – rather than masking it with anger – and learn ways of lowering the temperature in their rows.

Control/Rebellion

One half is valiantly trying to change the other; the other is valiantly trying to resist. Although the frustration is as great as for control/control couples, the atmosphere – at least on the surface – is much calmer. This is because the rebelling partner will agree to the plans of the controlling partner but then go out of their way to subvert them. Olivia wanted a new kitchen and as her husband, Ian, was a builder, it should have been reasonably straightforward. Although Ian agreed in principle, he had many private reservations. He did not want to spend his free time working. He thought his wife's choice was too expensive and he saw nothing wrong with their existing kitchen (which was only three years old). Instead of being honest and giving his true opinions, he side-stepped a possible disagreement and agreed to start 'soon'. Except each weekend, there was the Grand Prix or some important football fixture. Next, he spent some of their savings – without consultation – replacing his work van, and put off purchasing the kitchen units.

When Olivia's frustration reached fever pitch, he made a start and bought himself some time, but did not follow through. 'The kitchen looks like a bomb site,' complained Olivia. 'But everything's still working,' countered Ian. 'I'll get round to it – just give me time. It's not as if I feel encouraged by the atmosphere in the house.' Later, in counselling, he admitted he would sometimes pick an argument so he could storm out of the house and avoid the job.

At first glance, Ian might have seemed powerful but it was all negative power. He could thwart Olivia's desires but he was so busy digging in his heels that he had lost sight of what he wanted himself. (This behaviour is called passive-aggressive and there is more about it in the next chapter.) To resolve this pattern, the rebelling partner needs to realise that although he or she might avoid a row in the short term, this strategy causes much more aggravation in the medium and long term. Meanwhile, the controlling partner has to learn to be more flexible. After many weeks' discussion, Olivia agreed to some cheaper units – rather than her dream kitchen – and they negotiated a works schedule that suited both of them (not just Olivia).

The Alternative

In small doses, there is nothing wrong with any of these patterns for dealing with difference. Sometimes it is necessary for one half to make a decision and the other to go along with it (control/compliance) or to row about important issues (control/control). Likewise there are times when neither partner has the energy or inclination to get worked up over something (indifference/indifference). The problem is when a couple become stuck in one particular pattern or, worse still, retreat into more and more extreme versions. In the long term this behaviour will drain all the connection, all the understanding and, ultimately, all the love out of a relationship.

Fortunately, there is an alternative: open and honest communication – which leads to *cooperation/cooperation*.

Three Laws of Relationship Disputes

Before you can reach cooperation/cooperation, I need to lay out three fundamental ideas that will lower the stakes in your arguments, build bridges, and explain why seemingly small issues can become major sticking points.

Six of one and half a dozen of the other

This wisdom was always my mother's response when my sister and I fell out and tried to get her to take sides. In twenty-five years of relationship counselling, I have yet to meet a couple that do not share equal responsibility for their problems. (The exception is violent and abusive relationships or when someone is an addict.) From time to time, I hear such a persuasive story that I've been tempted to believe I've finally found an exception.

However, with a little digging, I always find that the story is not so black and white. Both sides have made an equal, if different, contribution to their unhappiness.

Unfortunately, our culture, and particularly the law, is determined to divide the innocent from the guilty. When we tell our friends, 'You'll never believe what he said to me' or 'Guess what she's done now', we edit the story for us to appear in the best possible light. We do not mention that we were two inches from our partner's face, screaming at the top of our voice, or conveniently forget our own mean and inconsiderate acts. As we reconstruct the fight, either in our heads or to anyone who will listen, we become more in the right and our partner more in the wrong. This process might make it easier for us to live with ourselves, but harder to live with each other.

What about adultery? Is that also six of one and half a dozen of the other? Certainly after an affair, society likes to label the 'guilty' party who cheated and the 'innocent' party who was cheated on. Yet in my experience, even here the circumstances are always much murkier. When Donna had an affair at work and her husband Denis found out, she was deeply ashamed and they came into counselling. 'What Denis won't listen to is the reasons why I felt tempted,' explained Donna. 'He had been so busy that it seemed he paid me no attention whatsoever. When this man at work noticed me, it was very tempting. He even seemed interested in what I was saying.' Before anything happened, Donna tried to talk to Denis and to plan more activities together, but Denis's most important contract was up for renewal. Tied up with his work, Denis did not even notice that she had embarked on an affair. Donna found this particularly upsetting: 'I'd make this extra special effort whenever I went out, and, of course, I was going out more often. My moods were all over the place – excited one minute, horrified with myself the next. Yet still Denis didn't twig.' Eventually she confessed to the affair and it ended. What Donna did was wrong, but Denis's behaviour was a contributing factor. Innocent? Guilty? Can anyone truly apportion blame? And ultimately, does it matter?

When all the 'but's, 'if's and 'extenuating circumstances' have been stripped away, the responsibility in every relationship dispute is pretty much fifty/fifty. Maybe someone could claim forty-eight/fifty-two, but a generosity of spirit – a very good asset in a relationship – would suggest that it is pointless to quibble.

Once 'six of one and half a dozen of the other' has been taken on board, couples are much less likely to fall into the trap of blaming during a nasty argument. After all, both halves have contributed to the problem.

EXERCISE: SIX OF ONE AND HALF A DOZEN OF THE OTHER

It is easier to spot when other couples are equally to blame than to accept equal responsibility in our own relationship. So while getting the hang of this idea, take a break from examining your life and look at a couple from a TV show, book or movie.

For example, Jane Austen created a timeless couple with Mr Darcy and Elizabeth Bennet. She even helped us spot their respective weaknesses by calling the book *Pride and Prejudice*. Austen carefully balanced her characters so that the misunderstandings and the obstacles to their happiness can be laid equally at both their feet. What about Jane Eyre and Mr Rochester, or Rhett Butler and Scarlett O'Hara? From the sitcom *Friends*, examine the responsibility of Rachel and Ross.

After a while, spotting the 'six of one and half a dozen of the other' for famous couples becomes easy; when this is the case, start applying the same test to your own relationship.

Emotional equals attract

When I trained as a relationship counsellor, I had found this idea of emotional equals attract hard to accept. Surely, in every relationship, one person is better at talking about their feelings, and doesn't that make them potentially better skilled with emotions? It is a widespread belief that one half of a partnership – normally a woman – is better at relationships. On many occasions one partner will bring the other to the counselling room with the implicit message: 'I'm fine, it's him/her who needs sorting out' (however, twenty-five years as a marital therapist has taught me to know better). It it soon becomes clear that both partners need the sessions – equally.

To explain the second law, it is important to understand what makes up an emotionally healthy individual. The first factor is an ability to be honest about and engage with feelings. Every family has its own problem topics handed down from one generation to the next – subjects that the family are so uncomfortable about that each member pretends they don't exist. Common examples would be sex, anger, money, competitiveness, sibling rivalry, jealousy – but the list is endless.

'When I was growing up, my mother would get all flustered whenever there was kissing on the TV,' said Terry, a twenty-nine-year-old plumber, 'and although I'd tease her about it, I've never really felt comfortable talking about sex, and, unlike mates at work, would never brag about conquests or make dirty jokes. It just doesn't feel right.'

Obviously, it is impossible for us to cut ourselves off from complicated emotions, so we ignore them. I think of it as like putting a screen up to hide an unpleasant view. As a rule of thumb, the fewer emotions hidden behind the screen, the more emotionally healthy the individual. Some people have low screens and find it easier to look behind at the difficult emotions; others have such high and thick screens that they are totally unaware of their off-limits subjects.

The second factor for emotional health is well-balanced boundaries. In some families, everybody is so in and out of each other's business that it becomes hard to know what problems or emotions belong to which family member. These low boundaries can be a problem as the children can grow into adults who do not respect their partner's need for privacy or grasp that he or she might have different viewpoints. Conversely, there are some families where the boundaries are so high that the members share virtually nothing; and these children grow into adults who shut their partners out.

On many occasions, someone who appears very good at talking about relationships turns out to be happy with only a narrow range of emotions. Meanwhile, their partner – who talks less but thinks deeper – may find it easier to delve into the difficult topics hidden behind the screen. Alternatively, the silent partner might be better at listening.

Whatever the different skills, screens and boundaries each half of the couple brings to the relationship, each, in fact, has a matching level of emotional maturity. Often the skills are complementary and the secret of relationship counselling is to get a couple pulling in the same direction.

An example of a relationship which seemed, on the surface, to be emotionally unbalanced is that of Carrie and Jay – in their fifties with two grown-up children. Carrie did most of the talking and whenever I asked Jay a question he would either shrug or tell me: 'I don't know.' That would be Carrie's cue for a long discussion on Jay's mother, his childhood and what he was feeling. Jay would sit there nodding. Carrie was certainly fluent in the language of feelings but became increasingly uncomfortable when the spotlight was turned on to her. Out of her mouth would come a barrage of words but afterwards, when I looked at my notes, it seemed that she had said nothing concrete. So, instead, I asked Jay to talk about Carrie's background and a few facts emerged. 'Carrie's mother was ill for much of her childhood and she used to lie on a divan in the living room,' he explained. 'I became her eyes and ears,' Carrie chipped in. Slowly they painted a picture of a little girl who would listen for hours to her mother's complaints and be her permanently on-call agony aunt. Carrie would bring her snippets of news from the family and neighbourhood and they would pore over the details together. 'It made me feel important, OK,' explained a more subdued Carrie.

Conversely, Jay came from a family where nobody ever talked about feelings. No wonder Carrie and Jay were attracted to each other. Jay found someone to discuss those forbidden feelings and Carrie found a partner for her ventriloquism act. This relationship had worked well at the beginning but Carrie had become more expressive and Jay quieter until – as is often the case – both started hating the other for the very quality that had first attracted them.

Finally, it was a question from Jay that provided the breakthrough: 'Did you and your mother ever talk about your relationship?' Carrie blustered. I kept quiet. 'It can't have been fun stuck inside with your mother when the other girls were out playing,' Jay added thoughtfully. Carrie had often analysed the family, but there were unspoken limits. Her own relationship with her mother, and the restraints it placed on Carrie, were completely taboo. Although Jay might have been more detached from his family, the distance had sharpened his perception. Both Carrie and Jay had their emotional strengths and weaknesses – in effect, equals had attracted.

'Emotional equals attract' is a very difficult philosophy to accept. I remember explaining it to a journalist who became very thoughtful. 'So what does it say about me that I've just had a short relationship with someone needy and paranoid?' she asked. I wished I had kept quiet. However, she decided to answer her own question: 'After my divorce, I suppose needy and paranoid just about summed me up.' Many people would have found it easier to blame the ex-partner than to look at themselves. Yet blaming our partner makes us disrespectful and cruel towards them, and ultimately produces destructive arguments.

Understanding that emotional equals attract makes people less likely to belittle each other. After all, each partner has just as many failings – and strengths – as the other.

EXERCISE: EMOTIONAL EQUALS ATTRACT

When something is hard to take on trust, it is a good idea to find evidence from your life experience. This exercise will help you explore the concept and provide a launch pad for thinking about your own relationship.

- Choose a couple that you know very well and have a chance to watch regularly. If your parents are still together, that would be ideal, but your partner's parents, a sibling and their partner, or a pair of friends will work equally well.
- Take a piece of paper, divide it in half and at the top of each half write the name of one of the partners.
- Think of the qualities that make for good relationships: expressive of feelings; keeps things in proportion; good listener; open to change; well-maintained boundaries; insightful; brave; forgiving; thoughtful; assertive; willing to compromise; affectionate; curious; self-aware; kind; ambitious; outgoing; reliable in a crisis.
- Allocate each quality above – and any more you come up with – under each partner's name. If both partners demonstrate the quality, put it down for both of them.

- If you wish, you can add character defects too – but this is not essential.
- Compare both halves. How well balanced are the couple? Does the partner who seems to have less on their list have any hidden qualities that are harder to spot?

The eighty/twenty rule

The stubborn issues that are really hard to resolve are nearly always 80 per cent about the past and only 20 per cent about today. This is because patterns set up in our childhood have a knock-on effect on our adult relationships. When Kitty passed her driving test in her mid-twenties, she couldn't understand why her partner's inability to drive became such a big issue. 'It had never bothered me before,' she said. However, when she was introduced to the idea that arguments can have roots back to child-hood, Kitty began to make connections. 'My dad started losing his sight when I was about three; in fact, my earliest memory was of his car being towed away after a nasty accident. From then onwards, my mother did all the driving and there were times when naturally she resented always being the one on soft drinks at parties.' For Kitty, her partner automatically leaping into the passenger seat had triggered past associations. Once she understood her feelings and explained them to her partner, driving became less of a flash point.

Another example of the eighty/twenty rule are Brian and Andy – a gay couple for whom taste and design caused rifts. They were most likely to fight over purchasing something for their house. The 20 per cent was about a natural-fibres rug for the living room, but the 80 per cent was about their backgrounds and their families' attitudes to money. Andy had been brought up in a middle-class family where money was plentiful, until his father's drinking got out of control and the business failed. From this experience, Andy learned to enjoy money while it was around. Meanwhile, Brian had come from a working-class family – with six brothers and sisters – where, although his father had a steady job, money was always tight. One of his strongest childhood memories was finding money on the beach, the pleasure of being able to give it to his mother, and the extra food it bought that week. Brian's lesson from his childhood was that money is scarce and should be hoarded. Although understanding the eighty/twenty rule did not settle whether Brian and Andy should have bought the rug, it did stop the dispute getting out of control or going round in circles.

Understanding the eighty/twenty rule will stop the same issues repeatedly coming up and an argument descending into bitterness.

EXERCISE: THE EIGHTY/TWENTY RULE

This concept is easier to come to grips with than the other exercises, so we will start closer to home.

- Make a list of the petty things about your partner that irritate you. For example: hanging around the house without getting dressed on their day off or leaving bills lying around the hallway.
- Now turn Sherlock Holmes on yourself and discover why these issues get your goat. What does each bad habit mean to you? What memories does each bring back? What would your mother or father say about these things? What would your previous boyfriends, girlfriends or partners have said?
- Next, think back to your childhood and come up with your earliest memory. How many details can you remember? Where were you standing; who else was there; what colours; what smells; any tastes; what about touching something; how did you feel? Once the memory is as vivid as possible, look for other childhood moments that might link in.

- Still playing detective, start to put together a case. Remember how detectives first try out a theory, mentally exploring the possibilities and then looking for evidence either to support the theory or knock it down. Take the same approach with the influences of your parents on your personality and your relationship issues. For example, Kitty – whose father lost his sight – could discover how frightening her first memory had been. At three, we are very dependent on our parents. She could then ask what impact this had on her choice of partners. Does she play safe with a very reliable man? Conversely, she might need to keep confronting her fears and choose the excitement of a dangerous man. Do not close down any line of enquiry without thinking it through and testing your gut reaction. This is hard, because we are naturally loyal to our parents, but the aim is to understand ourselves, not to blame them.

- Finally, think back to your parents' favourite sayings. They might be philosophical, for example: 'Life's not fair', 'Do as you would be done by' or 'There's no such word as can't'. Or, they might be personal: 'Why can't you be more like your brother?', 'Big boys don't cry', or 'Don't worry, you're the . . . [fill in the gap: pretty, clever, etc.] one'. Look at how much the drip, drip, drip of these sayings has marked your personality or view of the world. How many of the contentious issues with your partner are built on these opinions? Are they still true?

These questions will help you pinpoint the hidden 80 per cent of a current issue with your partner to which you might previously have been oblivious.

Where You Argue and What it Says About Your Relationship

After a row, when couples have a post-mortem, they pore over what was said and how they feel. The last thing they analyse is where the argument happened. Once when I got stuck with a couple and could not find a way to break through their bickering, I decided to take a different approach. I stopped asking what happened and asked where. The effect was miraculous. Instead of rehashing the issues, they took a step back and became more analytical. So I did some research with my other clients in order to discover where they argued and what the location said about their relationship.

The three most productive places for arguments

1. Car

It's not just back-seat driving, traffic jams and poor map-reading that make the car the place you are most likely to have a row. In our busy twenty-first-century lives, it is one of the few extended times that we spend with our partners. Unlike at home, it is hard to storm off when arguments get heated. Plus, with the driver's attention fixed on the road, we think a controversial issue might be easier to slip into general conversation. Certainly our partner will find it harder to spot if we are anxious, blushing or being devious. However, without direct eye contact, our body language and intentions are more likely to be misunderstood.

What it says about your relationship: With a driver and a passenger, nowhere are the issues of control and power more out in the open. Arguments in the car are really about who is in charge. Modern couples like to feel they are equal, but underneath the surface one half often feels powerless.

Solve it: In successful relationships control is divided. For example, one will be in charge of major spending decisions while the other organises the children. Draw up a list of activities, areas of the house and responsibilities and put down who has the final say by each. If the balance is uneven, discuss which areas can be passed over. Always consult your partner in your areas and be careful not to belittle their opinions.

2. Kitchen

This is mission control in any house and the place that couples are most likely to meet at stressful times – like first thing in the morning. The kitchen also throws up plenty of fuel for a row: washing-up left lying around, clothes not taken out of the tumble drier or using the last of the milk. If you have children, it often provides somewhere where you can hiss at each other away from prying ears – while they are busy watching TV in the living room or finishing their homework in their bedrooms.

What it says about your relationship: Do you really feel appreciated? At the bottom of many domestic arguments one or both partners feel taken for granted. However, rather than focus on the causes, many couples unwittingly concentrate on the small surface issues and beat themselves up because they believe the rows are out of all proportion.

Solve it: Compliments and 'thank you's are really important. Nobody can ever have enough praise. When first courting, we leave each other notes and buy surprise bars of chocolate – don't stop just because the relationship is established. Next time you tell your partner you love her or him, add on one of the reasons why. It might seem like a joke – 'because you make a great lasagne' – but it makes your love declaration seem less of a reflex and more grounded.

3. Out and about

Many couples deliberately discuss controversial subjects in coffee shops and restaurants. They feel it is harder to lose their tempers in public and hope witnesses will keep them both rational. Other couples row at parties after alcohol has loosened their tongues or because secretly each hopes friends or family will take their side. Finally, shopping with your partner is another opportunity for conflict.

What it says about your relationship: In these relationships, an argument is often seen as a failure. You try and be rational and many times convince yourself there is really nothing major to be angry about – so why upset the apple cart? However, a lot of feelings are being repressed.

Solve it: Understand that rows are part of a healthy relationship. Letting off steam can be the first step to solving a dispute. If you are going out to discuss issues so as to be away from the kids, think again. Hearing their parents bring up issues and solve them is the best way for children to learn how to do it themselves.

The three least productive places for arguments

1. Living room

The television is often the focus in the living room and an ever-present excuse not to engage: 'Could we talk about this later? I'm watching my programme.' Although generally a pacifier, TV can occasionally be the source of conflict. The jealous partner monitors whether the other is too interested in semi-clothed actresses or actors. Plot lines can also stand in for submerged issues: 'That's just the sort of thing you'd do.'

What it says about your relationship: Are you depersonalising any conflict, afraid that it will get out of hand? However, talking about issues second hand – through the soaps – takes the argument out of your hands into the scriptwriters'.

Solve it: Instead of backing up your case with other people's opinions – what your friends or family think – own the opinions. 'I don't like it when you put your feet on the sofa' rather than: 'My friend was disgusted when she saw you slobbing out.' This will stop your partner becoming defensive and make him or her more likely to hear what you have to say.

2. Bedroom

Couples are more likely to kiss and make up than row in the bedroom. Although different levels of desire can cause tension, sex in general is such a difficult subject couples repress rather than talk over the issues. If the relationship is in crisis, one partner will often go up earlier and pretend to be asleep when the other comes to bed.

What it says about your relationship: Arguing in the bedroom is a sure sign that you are overtired. Tension at bedtimes will make sleep more difficult and further exacerbate the problem. How good is your love life? Has an OK sex life drifted into something boring and unfulfilling?

Solve it: Look at your priorities. Are you taking on too much? How can you change your evenings to give more time to talk and solve problems? Don't be afraid to also set aside time for lovemaking – so sex is no longer the last effort of an exhausted mind and body.

3. Garden

It is not the soothing effect of nature that makes this the place couples are least likely to fight. Arguing in public is embarrassing enough without having to face witnesses the next day and, unlike family, neighbours are particularly unforgiving and prone to gossiping.

What it says about your relationship: These arguments are out of control and a sign that a couple can't live together but can't let go. They promise that next time round everything will be better, but soon fall into the same old pattern.

Solve it: Agreeing to try harder is not enough. Step back and really understand what drives your arguments and why they have become so destructive.

Summing Up

Every relationship has problems; it is how you deal with them that is important. Misunderstandings, problems and rows are 'six of one and half a dozen of the other'; by taking this on board couples will stop blaming each other. The second law of relationship disputes – emotional equals attract – shows that not only do both halves of a couple have equal skills to draw on to solve a row, but that these skills are normally complementary. If a dispute seems insoluble, look at how the 80 per cent from the past is driving the 20 per cent from today.

IN A NUTSHELL:
- Take stock: what drives your arguments?
- Identify your good and unhelpful habits. What would you like to change?
- Find a middle way. Having no rows can be just as harmful as having too many.

STEP 2

LOW-CONFLICT
RELATIONSHIPS

No nasty rows, no falling out, and no bitterness – it sounds wonderful, but is it really possible to completely transcend the tensions and live blissfully ever after? In reality, arguing is an important part of a healthy partnership; it uncovers the issues that really matter and enables partners to distinguish between minor irritations and serious problems. An argument creates the impetus to speak out, cuts through excuses, and finally creates a sense that 'something must be done'. Although rows sometimes make us uncomfortable, sometimes that can be good.

So why are some people afraid to let rip with their loved ones? The first reason for being less confrontational is the trend for couples to be each other's best friends as well as lovers. It's considered bad form for friends to scream at each other;

friends should be supportive, understanding and, most importantly, accept us as we are. 'My husband has a terrible habit of interrupting people,' says Kate, a thirty-two-year-old market researcher. 'His best man even joked about it in his wedding speech. I've tried teasing him but he says I knew his failings when I married him. So now I have to bite my lip.'

Couples with children can be especially nervous of having rows. 'Not in front of the children' is the buzzword for a generation that is ultra cautious about undermining their sons' and daughters' confidence or causing other psychological problems. And, with children being allowed to stay up later as they get older, 'not in front of the children' is soon transformed into seldom arguing at all. This is a pity because when children witness a constructive argument, they learn important lessons about honesty, compromise and reconciliation.

Another reason is that couples are simply too nice to argue. In many of these partnerships, one or both halves have watched their parents get divorced and are only too aware how apocalyptic a row can be. 'The day we got married, I told Jim: "I'll discuss, I'll listen, but I won't fight",' says Lydia, a fifty-nine-year-old dental technician.

'I watched my father and mother fight incessantly, and it's no way to live.' In an insecure world, where work is forever restructured and our extended families live further apart, our relationships are more important than ever. Therefore, is it any wonder that we play safe and avoid the conflict?

Busy work schedules mean that couples spend less time together. On the most simplistic level, if you hardly see each other you have fewer opportunities to fight. But it goes deeper. Just as overworked parents stress the importance of 'quality time' with their children, couples want what little time they do spend together to be perfect. Not only does this expectation put pressure on a couple to get the most out of their shared leisure time, but it also makes them less inclined to express their dissatisfaction. 'Our only concentrated time together is on holiday or weekends away,' explains Kate's partner, Robert, a thirty-five-year-old software salesman. 'After splashing out thousands to fly to the Maldives, I was not going to let myself get jealous about the way Kate flirted with the staff.' It takes sustained time together to feel relaxed enough to let down your barriers and be open about your grievances. When does a two-career couple have that?

The changing nature of the workplace is another culprit in making us less likely to argue. New management techniques have done away with old-fashioned confrontation in favour of finding consensus, and this is making itself felt at home as well as in the office. Michael is a forty-year-old manager with London Underground whose wife, Sue, noticed a marked difference after a particular training course. 'He decided we could only make a point if we were holding the talking stick – a wooden spoon from the kitchen,' she explains. 'I wanted to clock him with it. But every time I lost my temper he would calmly say things like "I hear your anger" and "We won't get closure this way". I had to keep telling him "I'm not one of your middle managers".' As Sue discovered, it takes two to make an argument.

Some younger high-flying couples – particularly those in their twenties – feel an immense pressure to be perfect. These individuals may have excelled in school, attended the best universities and colleges, graduated into exciting or high-paid jobs and are now buying their own homes. The perfect relationship is another box to tick and, sadly, arguments do not fit into that profile. Michelle, a twenty-seven-year-old TV researcher, speaks for many who strive for perfection: 'I would have been mortified if any of our friends had known that Claude and I were having relationship problems.' Michelle was very concerned about achieving and worried if any of her contemporaries were promoted in case she was falling behind – and her marriage had become part of this competition. Unfortunately, this couple had played the game so well that even Michelle was not aware of any serious difficulties until her husband disappeared for two months and reappeared on the other side of the world.

Other couples do not argue because one half is so keen to help the other grow that they almost become their personal therapist or guru. How can you complain about that? After all, it is done out of the best possible motive . . . 'I just want the best for you.' However, these well-intentioned partners can soon be telling their other halves how to feel. Martin, a forty-two-year-old financial consultant found himself in this position: 'My father had died and I was in shock. I thought he'd always be there for me. How could this have happened? I just wanted to sit quietly in the car and get my head straight. However, all the way through the four-hour car journey home, my wife kept on at me: "You've got to get this out."' There is a short step from trying to help someone to controlling them.

However, underlying all the above reasons for not arguing is one unifying fear: what will happen if a row gets out of control? My clients confess: 'Often I'd like to get angry but I'm frightened I'll never stop', or 'If I let it out, will I go completely nuts?', or 'Will he think less of me?'/'What if she rejects me?' Of course, these are all perfectly reasonable concerns – especially for someone who has seldom let go before. Other couples have argued in the past but have had bad experiences: 'When she loses her temper she shouts me down and I hate it,' they say, or 'If I get angry he blanks me for days afterwards and the atmosphere is horrible.'

TOP TEN TOPICS COUPLES ARGUE ABOUT

Over the past five years, I have been keeping a tally of what sparks rows. If you are in a low-conflict relationship, it is particularly helpful to know what provokes other people. How many of these issues sound familiar?

1. **Time.** Always in short supply. No wonder we often complain that our partner hasn't got enough for us.
2. **Feeling appreciated.** When we're tired, we take each other for granted. Also we're far

more likely to communicate what we dislike about our partner than what we like.

3. **Jealousy.** The modern disease. It can range from looking too long at a pretty face in the street to adultery.

4. **Money.** Different spending priorities are always difficult, but the new twist is discovering your partner has accumulated large credit card debts.

5. **Chores.** Not only who does what, but also how long it takes to get round to it. Whose turn it is to empty the dishwasher and how it was stacked in the first place are popular sparring topics.

6. **Sex.** One partner has 'gone off' sex – leaving the other bewildered and angry.

7. **Children.** Different ideas about discipline and what is appropriate at which age. For example: pre-teens wanting to dress provocatively.

8. **Computer.** Not just how much time is spent on the Internet – for work or pleasure – but developing deep 'friendships' in cyberspace and, in particular, looking at pornography.

9. **Space.** Traditionally it's been men who've wanted time to themselves, but women burdened by work and kids are asking for 'me' time too.

10. **In-laws.** Nobody likes unasked-for advice, especially when it comes from his or her parents.

Why Arguing is Good for Your Relationship

Couples like to think that they have integrity and generally tell each other the truth. One partner might pretend, for example, that the new home cinema cost a little less, or the other forgets to mention the stripper at their best friend's hen party, but there are few serious transgressions. Yet when it comes to our feelings, the rules change. We constantly tell white lies to preserve the peace or avoid upsetting our partner. How often have you said: 'No problem', 'Of course, I don't mind', 'It's nothing', when actually you meant the complete opposite? Often a couple will boast: 'We can tell each other anything' but in reality they tell each other close to nothing. Although the truth, both saying it and hearing it, can be scary, emotional honesty will set your relationship free and save it from becoming more and more dull.

The post-sixties generation no longer considers sex dirty, bad, or something embarrassing to be hidden away. Today's forbidden feeling is anger. Except, like sex, anger is a part of being a human and cannot be wished away. Whether we like to admit it or not, everybody gets angry at some time. Unfortunately, many couples are uncomfortable or frightened by anger and therefore develop strategies for keeping conflict at bay. However, all the avoidance strategies not only fail to deal with the underlying anger but ultimately cause more pain than dealing with the anger head-on.

Four common avoidance strategies are detachment, skipping, rationalising and blocking.

Detachment

Couples tell themselves: 'It doesn't matter', 'We'll agree to differ' and 'Ultimately, who cares?' While putting anger in cold storage can work in the short term, this strategy risks freezing over every feeling – even the positive ones.

The effect is devastating. Jennifer is a forty-year-old maritime lawyer: 'There were things I didn't agree with, important things, but I didn't want to rock the boat. So I didn't say anything, I just shut down, and gradually all my emotions became dulled.' Jennifer woke up one day in a passionless marriage and drifting towards divorce without knowing what was wrong. 'The whole focus of our counselling was on teaching us how to argue productively,' Jennifer explains. 'Although nothing was solved when we were shouting at each other, later, when we'd calmed down and had a civilised conversation, we always found a compromise.' The round-table discussions were productive because they had been through a cathartic conflict first. However, this is tough and many couples find themselves trapped in a vicious circle. By not arguing and processing anger, partners will become withdrawn and less likely to communicate – until the only strategy left is to detach.

LEARN TO NAME YOUR FEELINGS

Many clients claim not to have many feelings, but the reality is that they are not always aware of their full range. At first, some clients look blank when I ask them to write down as many feelings as possible. But then I bring in a flip-chart and, before long, we have filled a complete sheet.

1. **How many feelings can you list?** Write as many as you can on a piece of paper and then try and think of some more.

2. **Look at the range of your feelings.** Feelings belong in 'families', so circle and connect ones that you think belong together. In my opinion there are probably eight of these families:

Shock (including surprise, confusion, amazement)

Anger (including rage, resentment, frustration, annoyance, irritation, impatience)

Sadness (including grief, disappointment, hurt, despair)

Fear (including anxiety, worry, insecurity, panic, jealousy, guilt, shame)

Love (including acceptance, admiration, appreciation, gratitude, relief, empathy, compassion, sexiness)

Disgust (including contempt, disdain, aversion, scorn, revulsion)

Happiness (including joy, fulfilment, satisfaction, pleasure, contentment, amusement)

Numbness (including disconnected, blank, on auto-pilot, comfortable, empty, chilled)

However, you might find more families or decide some emotions belong in different places. There are no right or wrong choices. Maybe even invest in a thesaurus, because the richer the range of emotions the richer the life.

3. **Understand the complexity of your feelings.**
    So many of these feelings seem negative – five whole families (shock, anger, sadness, fear,

disgust), in fact — and the 'love' and 'happiness' families are often overlooked during our original brainstorm. Finally the 'numbness' family might seem safe, but do you want to spend your whole life here? The negative families can have positive sides; for example, there is always passion along with jealousy. Meanwhile, the positive ones have a downside; admiration, for example, can become unblinkered hero worship.

Skipping

Some couples accept that they will get angry, but because they also feel guilty or uncomfortable, push their anger away as quickly as possible. Anger is normally a wake-up call that something is wrong, but instead of listening to the message hidden beneath the pain, these couples skip straight to solving the dispute.

Jackie would get home later than her partner, Frank, and immediately start preparing the evening meal. If she was late, she would ask him to help chop up vegetables or cube meat. Although Frank was willing to help, it nearly always ended up with one or other of them getting angry. Sometimes she would skip the row by trying to second-guess what his problem might be. 'No wonder you're so slow – that knife needs sharpening,' she would tell him, or 'You're fed up because your favourite chopping board is still in the dishwasher.' Alternatively, he would try and solve the problem on the spot: 'You've had a hard time at work, go and put your feet up.' As soon as anger appeared on the scene, Frank and Jackie tried to avoid the argument by heading for the exit sign. These suggestions might have been made with love, but by skipping over the anger, they had found only superficial answers.

In counselling we unpacked the layers beneath chopping boards and tiredness. Jackie felt that a good wife should have prepared a hot meal by a certain time; Frank was able to reassure her that he was more flexible. However, there was more to their rows than this – ultimately, the couple had very rigid ideas of what men and women did in a relationship. Nevertheless, Jackie felt that she was doing the lion's share of the household chores and wanted more help. Meanwhile, Frank feared that she wanted to order him around – rather like his site supervisor at work. Although he was willing to do more at home, he did not want the same dynamics as at work. By no longer skipping the anger, Jackie and Frank discovered the layers of the argument and a proper solution.

KEEP A FEELINGS DIARY

For a week, whenever you have a spare few minutes, jot down any feeling that you have experienced. It could be on the train, when your next appointment is running late, or watching your kids playing. Write down all your feelings, even the ones that make you uncomfortable – in fact, especially those. This is a private diary, so be emotionally honest with yourself. You don't have to do anything with these feelings, just be aware of them and practise naming them.

When we are unsure of our emotions, we try to keep them down at the mild end of the spectrum for fear of being overwhelmed. Yet most people feel something a notch or two up from what they first report. So next time you write down, for example, that you are upset, try to be more honest and move further up the scale to the hidden emotions like anxiety, disappointment or frustration.

Looking back over your diary entries ask yourself, am I experiencing a wide range of feelings: shock, anger, sadness, fear, love, disgust, happiness? If one family is particularly under-represented, it is important to understand why. Did your parents have trouble experiencing these feelings? Why should you be inhibited? Next, deliberately look out for these emotions – even if they all come from the mild end. For example, if you feel very little from the love/happiness families, make certain you record the small pleasures. If you see a beautiful flower or smile at a cartoon in the paper write down 'happy' or 'content'.

Rationalising

While feelings are generally located in the body – for example, love seems to be an ache in the chest and fear a sinking sensation in the stomach – rationalising keeps everything logical, plausible and in the head.

Nick and Anna sought counselling after he fell out of love with her. They preferred to describe their arguments as 'heated discussions' and tried to neutralise any dispute by questioning each other's logic rather than addressing any underlying anger. A typical example would be the time Nick elbowed Anna in bed during the night. 'He attacked me,' she complained. 'I hardly think "attacked",' countered Nick, 'that suggests an element of premeditation.' Anna was straight back with: 'I'm not allowed to have an opinion now?' Their feelings were not being addressed as the argument quickly became about language, all conducted in the most reasonable and rational voices. By Nick and Anna's standards it was a nasty fight, but they were both still unsatisfied and quietly seething.

So we started to unpack the real issues. The elbow in the back, during a restless night, symbolised what Anna saw as Nick's uncaring attitude. But because she wanted him to stay, she was determined to be 'sweetness and light'. The feelings still had to come out somehow, and this 'heated discussion' was a subconscious attempt by Anna to deal with some of the frustration. If they had both lost their tempers, Anna would probably have blurted out the truth about holding back her feelings. By keeping everything very rational, they were protecting themselves from not only raised voices but also a proper understanding of their relationship's dynamics and a lasting solution.

DISTINGUISH BETWEEN FEELINGS AND THOUGHTS

Just putting 'I feel' at the beginning of a sentence doesn't make someone emotionally honest. For example: 'I feel you were wrong', or 'I feel you were out of order.' Both sentences tell us nothing about the emotions of the person talking. We could guess disappointment, perhaps, but maybe frustration or even contempt. What the speaker has expressed is an opinion.

1. **Thoughts come from our head.** They are opinions, ideas, judgements and beliefs. This does not make them any less valid but they are not feelings.

2. **Feelings often come from our body.** We have a physical reaction: a tightening of the chest; a sinking in the stomach; the heart beating faster; trembling.

3. **Communicate the feelings.** Once you have become fluent in identifying and naming feelings in your diary, move on to expressing them to your partner. Sometimes just acknowledging the feeling to yourself will make you less on edge. In some cases, you will no longer even feel the need to tell your partner, but if you do decide to tackle them, make certain to follow the next point.

4. **Own the feeling.** 'I feel' rather than 'You make me feel'. For example, 'I feel [angry, infuriated, frustrated, etc.] when you [keep leaving plastic bottles by the back door for me to put into the recycling box].' Not 'You make me angry with your thoughtlessness.' The more specific the complaint, the less it

> seems like an attack on someone's person-
> ality. After all, it is much easier to change our
> behaviour – putting out the plastic bottles –
> than our personality.

Blocking

One half gets angry, but the other half simply refuses to engage with their anger. The blocking partner will walk away, bury himself or herself in work and household chores, or just hide behind watching TV or reading the paper. Generally, Sian and Steven could solve their differences, but there was one topic that completely overwhelmed their coping skills. Steven had two large dogs, which had been specially bred to retrieve objects from water, and at the weekend he would be off at competitions. Sian was not a dog person and certainly not a large, wet, hairy dog person, so the dogs lived in a kennel outside. However, the potential for disagreements about Steven's hobby were endless. If Sian ever tried to tackle him about them, Steven would either be silent and just let her rant or walk out of the room. Sian would be left fuming – brimming over with anger. Although Steven would get angry, and perhaps slam a door, none of it would be expressed directly to Sian.

LISTENING ATTENTIVELY

In the same way that you expect your partner to be attentive to your feelings, be prepared to offer the same respect back.

1. Do not interrupt, try to minimise your partner's feelings, or tell him or her not to feel that way.

2. Acknowledge what has been said, even if it has been hard to hear. A responsible way to handle this, without taking all the blame, would be: 'I feel sad that you say that I . . .'

3. Remember: a greater awareness of feelings leads to a richer life with not only a better understanding of yourself but also better empathy with your partner and improved people skills all round.

Unprocessed Anger

Some people are so determined to mask their anger – because 'good people don't get mad' – that it has nowhere to go but inwards. Ultimately, the anger turns into headaches, ulcers, nervous conditions, depression or self-harm. The other costs of masked anger are not getting what you want and low self-respect.

If anger is not expressed, or swallowed, it will begin to seep out. Instead of direct criticism – which could either be challenged or maybe taken on board and acted on – there are snide comments and put-downs. Jilly, a forty-five-year-old marketing assistant, found low-grade resentment was ruining her life: 'He'd make sarcastic comments like "wonderful" and "of course, Princess" when I wanted, for example, to go out with my girlfriends. But if I challenged him, he'd just say something like: "Can't I even have an opinion now?" It was impossible to pin him down. Did he object to my night on the town, what I was wearing, or was he just jealous? Who knows? We'd just end up bickering all the time.' Behind each sarcastic comment are several unspoken opinions and again so many different layers. Is it any wonder neither party knows what they are really discussing or where they truly stand?

Instead of directly confronting issues some people either consciously or unconsciously play games. It is sneaky anger because, on the surface, they seem cooperative but they never get round to what they were asked. They 'forget' to make phone calls, put off DIY projects to next weekend or deliberately load the dishwasher incorrectly – so their partner does not ask again. Psychologists call this sort of behaviour passive-aggressive. While positive anger explodes and clears the air, passive aggression hangs around poisoning a relationship. As children, these people were often told not to yell, talk back, lose their temper, argue or rebel. In effect, their parents were saying: 'Let's pretend these feelings and impulses don't exist in me and I'll pretend they don't exist in you.'

Passive-aggressive adults always have a million excuses which make the real issues become harder and harder to tackle. Mark, a thirty-seven-year-old local government officer, would agree to do something for his partner but actually felt anything but cooperative: 'I'd smile to her face and agree "Of course it was my turn to empty the laundry basket", but I'd never quite get round to doing it. I was blowed if she was going to boss me about.' Eventually his partner retaliated and stopped doing things for him too. Having reached stalemate, they started counselling, and Mark learned to be honest about his feelings, rather than sneakily hiding his anger away. Finally, they could negotiate properly who did what, rather than snipe at each other. Other games played by the passive-aggressive include: 'Oops, I forgot'; 'Yes, but . . .' (add your own excuse), acting dumb and helpless and sulking. In the meantime, the other partner's patience snaps and he or she loses their temper. The passive-aggressive person will then turn self-righteous and blame their partner for the upset.

HOW TO DEAL WITH A PASSIVE AGGRESSOR

1. Ask yourself, why can't my partner assert himself or herself directly? Passive aggression is normally the choice of people who feel power-less. Is your partner allowed to say no?

2. Bring the hidden hostility up to the surface. Challenge any too-easy agreement: 'I don't think you want to . . .' Don't feel guilty or allow yourself to be manipulated into apologising for having got angry or annoyed.

3. Avoid misunderstandings. Repeat back instructions, set precise deadlines and at work establish penalties for procrastination.

4. Once you've made a stand, follow through. If someone is always late and you've told them you'll leave if they are more than ten minutes late and haven't called, then make certain

you do. Failure to carry out the penalties will severely weaken your position.

HOW TO STOP BEING PASSIVELY AGGRESSIVE

1. Accept that anger is normal.

2. Accept that you can still be a good person even when you feel angry.

3. Look at the benefits of using anger well. It gets things done and rights wrongs.

4. Understand your fears about being angry. What is the worst that could happen? What strategies could you use that will allow you to be angry but circumnavigate these fears?

5. Old behaviours, even if they worked for you as a child, will need updating. Unlike a kid, who has to go to school whether they like it or not, you have choices.

6. Practise saying no. It cuts through a lot of passive-aggressive behaviour. If there is a row at least both of you know what you are fighting

about, instead of your anger being masked by
sneaky behaviour.

7. Tell your partner when you feel pushed around.

Breaking Free From a Low-conflict Relationship

Having looked at the pain and problems caused
by denying arguments, it is time to turn and look
at constructive arguments. When I explain this
concept to my clients, one partner will often say:
'This is all very well, but I don't want to just pick
a fight.' The other will chip in: 'It all seems so
artificial.' So let's be clear. I am not suggesting
becoming needlessly confrontational or having
arguments for the sake of arguments. Every day
we are given invitations to get angry: someone
cuts in front of the car; our call is not returned;
we are given unfair criticism. What I ask is next
time an argument is brewing, don't side-step it.

Some clients, who are very uncomfortable with
conflict, start gently either with strangers or work
colleagues. Jackie, who avoided arguments over
preparing the evening meal, could feel herself getting
angry with a shop assistant who was too busy talking

to a colleague to serve her. 'Normally I would stand there and fume inside,' she explained, 'but this time I could feel my teeth clenching and I thought, go for it. I was surprised how calm I sounded when I said: "Excuse me, could you help me?"' The second surprise for Jackie was that there was no smart comment or comeback from the assistant. 'It turned out to be no big deal,' she told me. After practising on strangers, she was ready to be honest with Frank too. Jackie might have recognised her invitation to get angry, but many couples have become so adept at avoiding issues that they forget the signs.

THE SEVEN SIGNS THAT YOU NEED AN ARGUMENT

Look at the list below and ask yourself: How many invitations to be angry have I ignored?

1. One partner is more silent than usual.

2. Body language: not looking each other in the eye; hunched shoulders; crossed arms; tense jaw; tapping your foot or pacing around.

3. Voice pitch changes: tension in the vocal cords makes them tighter and the sounds more brittle.

4. Taking offence easily: 'Why did you do that?'

5. Repeatedly checking with each other: 'Are you OK?', 'Everything all right?' – but receiving a sharp or irritated response.

6. Pointless contradicting: 'No, I don't agree', 'Are you sure?'

7. Things that you have put up with for ages, without complaint, suddenly start grating.

Summing Up

Arguments are necessary for solving the inevitable conflicts between two people in a loving relationship. However, many couples are frightened of having rows in case they spin out of control. Destructive strategies for keeping anger at bay include detachment, skipping, rationalising and blocking. Unfortunately, trying to avoid anger can cause more problems than just letting rip.

IN A NUTSHELL:

- Be open and honest about your feelings. It is the foundation for good communication.
- Ducking an invitation to argue might be easier in the short term but it stores up problems for the future.
- Although rows are never nice, they do provide an opportunity to solve long-standing issues.

STEP 3

HIGH-CONFLICT
RELATIONSHIPS

Anger is a double-edged sword. On one side, it is a gift – providing the energy to get things done, redress injustice and sort out problems. On the other, anger can get us into a lot of trouble. Understanding the differences and harnessing the positive elements of anger is one of the most important relationship skills; unfortunately, it is also one of the most difficult.

There are two types of high-conflict relationship couples who seek my help. For the first group, anger has always been a problem – either the couple fight like cat and dog or one partner is almost permanently angry and the other tiptoeing round the next row. For the second group, there is a particular unsolved problem that has turned nasty and consumed all the goodwill until it is impossible to talk about anything without the conversation degenerating into threats, name-calling and one partner getting upset, making the other upset, which, in turn, makes the first partner even more upset, and so on. Even the happiest relationships sometimes have arguments where anger gets out of hand and one partner (but normally both) gets hurt. So what is the answer?

The best place to start is by understanding the differences between the positive and negative sides of anger. Healthy anger is when we recognise a real problem, act on it and then let it go once the issue is resolved. Most importantly, the anger is also in proportion to the offence. In sharp contrast, anger becomes a problem when someone represses it (because they can't deal with it) and then explodes with rage (getting angrier than is appropriate or necessary) or likes anger too much (because it makes them feel powerful and helps them get their own way). While there is only one type of healthy anger – more about this at the end of the chapter – there are six types of negative anger, which are listed below. After each one, there is an exercise specifically designed to help you break out of this anger style.

Sudden Anger

This kind of anger arrives quickly and dissipates quickly. Although these people get rid of their frustrations, they end up saying terrible things. Once they have cooled down, and registered the reactions and impact on their nearest and dearest, they feel ashamed, guilty and determined not to let it happen again – until the next time. So what's going on?

Because people prone to sudden anger do not like anger in themselves or others, they ignore the triggers that make everybody else annoyed. However, instead of dealing with the issues, they grit their teeth, deny their feelings and carry on. Except that the feelings do not disappear; the frustration and the pressure build up to such an intolerable level that they explode.

For example, Virginia would, as her partner Gordon described it, go ballistic. She would yell, swear and even throw things – like the breakfast bowl he'd put in the sink rather than in the dishwasher. Inside his head, Gordon would dismiss his partner as 'a moody cow'. But because Virginia had denied all the previous irritations, Gordon was not aware of the thousand other things that had broken down her composure – just the final straw. From his viewpoint, her anger had no rhyme or reason: 'I'd forgotten to put my bowl away hundreds of times before and she'd not reacted like that – totally out of all proportion to the crime.' Most people with sudden anger issues have high – almost unrealistic – standards for themselves (taking on so much that they are easily stressed) and for other people.

How to recognise it

Everybody loses their temper from time to time, but you have a problem when:

- You get angry over 'stupid' or petty things that you would generally take in your stride. Worse still, your anger seems to come out of nowhere and it is only in retrospect that you can identify the pressure points.
- Instead of feeling better that issues are out in the open, you feel worse, guilty or stupid and your partner and family are upset.
- Your body language can turn very aggressive. You tap your feet, start pacing, keep sighing, try to work faster (to distract yourself) and start slamming things down.
- When someone asks 'What's the matter?', this will raise rather than lower the tension.

- Instead of solving problems, your anger has become one of the stumbling blocks.

SLOWING DOWN YOUR ANGER

Instead of going from nought to one hundred in a few seconds, slow down your reactions, understand the triggers better and head off the worst of the crisis.

Monitor your body: Become aware of the tension in your head, neck and shoulders. What's happening in your stomach or across your chest? Have your eyes narrowed? What about your hands or feet? Has your voice changed? How?

Keep an anger diary: Write down everything that is making you angry or has made you angry in the run-up to a sudden explosion. What are the patterns? How do you describe yourself in your private thoughts: A victim? A saint? Have you jumped to conclusions? Do you feel people deserve your anger?

Deal with the stress: Breathe slowly and deeply. Relax your face and body. Stop pacing. Tell yourself to calm down. Check that you are using your normal voice. Let the anger drain away.

Take responsibility: It is your job to avoid an explosion – not other people's to calm you down. How can you soothe yourself? What makes you feel better? Going for a walk? A round of golf? Having a bath? Cleaning?

Resolve the issue: When you have cooled down, look at the triggers and find the fundamental problems that are driving your anger. Once out of the red zone, it is tempting to side-step or downgrade problems, but this just provides fuel for the next outburst. Instead, use the skills in the next chapter to talk to your partner and resolve any outstanding issues.

Habitual Anger

These people are constantly angry and, most of the time, cannot put their finger on exactly why. Many people with habitual anger will always have been grumpy, irritated quickly and generally on a short fuse. They learned as children that tantrums got their parents' attention; they might not necessarily have got what they wanted but even negative attention was better than none at all. More commonly, habitual anger is a sign that a relationship has been in trouble for a long time. Nothing seems to resolve any of the couple's problems and they settle down into trench warfare where anything can set off another round of fire and afterwards each partner retreats to the relative safety of their bunkers.

Rebecca was angry all the time with her partner, Daniel, and vice versa. In order to break the deadlock, I facilitated a discussion about finding one nice thing that each could do for the other. Daniel would have liked a cup of tea in the morning. 'It's not fair, I have to get up early and I haven't got time to run around after him,' Rebecca replied. There followed a debate about whether she could switch on the kettle before she left – so it would be ready when Daniel came down. 'But what if the kettle was empty? I'm really pressed for time,' she complained. 'So you can't even do that,' said Daniel. 'I knew you'd turn this into another stick to beat me,' countered Rebecca.

Daniel had just as many excuses for his nice thing for Rebecca – buying bread for her sandwiches – and it soon became clear this conversation was going nowhere. 'What are you both so angry about?' I asked. They paused for a moment, perplexed, and then launched into a list of complaints, but they weren't answering my question. They were too habitually angry to look beneath the surface.

How to recognise it

You can tell your anger has turned into a habit when:

- It feels normal to be angry and outbursts happen almost automatically these days.
- You feel pessimistic most of the time and especially about your partner's ability to change.
- You have high expectations of other people and they generally let you down.
- You are too mad, too quickly and for too long.

THE ANGER PYRAMID

The best way to stop anger being an automatic habit is by understanding what fuels it and how different issues interlock.

1. Imagine an upside-down pyramid filled with things that make you angry.

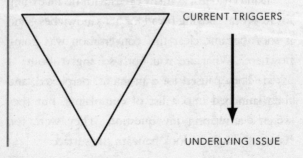

CURRENT TRIGGERS

UNDERLYING ISSUE

Across the top are all the current triggers – for example, Rebecca and Daniel would put *buying bread* or *making tea*.

2. What drives those immediate issues goes in the layer underneath and so on.

3. To get down from the multitude of minor issues at the top, to the overriding issue at the bottom, take one of the immediate triggers and ask:

   'Why does [for example] making tea in the morning make me angry?'

   Rebecca answered: *Because I have to get up so early*.

4. Take your answer and repeat the question:

   'Why does . . . *getting up early* . . . make me angry?'

   Rebecca answered: *Because he's still lying in bed*.

5. Keep repeating the process:

'Why does . . . *Daniel lying in bed* . . . make me angry?'

Rebecca answered: *Because I have to work so hard.*

'Why does . . . *working so hard* . . . make me angry?'

Rebecca answered: *Because I have to earn the lion's share of the money.*

'Why does . . . *earning the lion's share* . . . make me angry?'

6. Stop when you find something new or surprising:

   Rebecca answered: *I want to give up work and have a baby.*

7. Turn this discovery from a statement into a question:

   How can we afford to have a baby?

   Rebecca and Daniel finally had the underlying issue driving their habitual anger and instead of scrapping over trivia could really begin to talk.

Shame-based Anger

These people have a low opinion of themselves. Their parents, teachers and society in general have given them the message that they are not 'good enough'. Fortunately, they have found a way of coping day-to-day with this pain. Unfortunately, it is making the situation worse. So what is happening?

First, they deny how they feel deep down and cover up by being either arrogant ('I'm better than everybody else') or perfectionists ('I can only feel good about myself if I'm perfect'). Unfortunately, people suffering from shame-based anger can never quite persuade themselves that they really are better than anybody else, so even the slightest criticism brings their whole act tumbling down. These are the people who, if you correct a spelling mistake, will explode and flounce off: 'If you don't want my help . . .' They have such a poor opinion of themselves that anything less than a standing ovation seems like a rebuke. It also goes without saying that nobody can be perfect all the time. So there is a lot of fuel for anger being carried about.

Some people turn the destructive feeling inwards (like self-harming or self-sabotage) but more commonly, and this is the second problem with this coping strategy, they take it out on other people. As a child, Simon felt his mother preferred his brother and indeed she often said he would 'never amount to anything'. As an adult, Simon was naturally very sensitive to criticism. In his first counselling session, he listed some of the incentive trips and prizes that he had won as salesman of the month. The couple had financial problems – since Amanda had given up working after the birth of their second child – and if the subject of money came up, Simon would immediately start bristling: 'I follow up every lead, I'm even on the phone in the evening trying to earn more commission.' Amanda would try and clarify: 'I'm just saying we have to decide on our spending priorities.' It was too late, Simon was straight into attack mode: 'What about the state of the house? It's no pleasure to come home to toys all over the place and nappy-changing stuff in the middle of the living room. It's not hygienic . . .' Simon believed it was better to attack than be attacked and on many occasions, it worked – Amanda was scared off and left him alone. Unfortunately, it was also ruining his marriage.

How to recognise it

This is a fault easier to recognise in other people than in ourselves – and I meet many couples where both partners are equally guilty – so look at the following and ask whether you have fallen into the shame-based anger trap too:

- You judge yourself so harshly, you expect other people to do the same. Can you hear criticism when none was intended? Do you overreact?
- Do you ever wonder that if someone knew the 'real you' they would stop loving or abandon you? (By trying to cover up your supposed faults, you are actually becoming unlovable and feeding your fears of being abandoned.)
- Shame and blame have become inextricably linked.
- You keep a mental score sheet and feel powerful in victory and overwhelmed when defeated. For this reason, compromises are hard to find.
- When challenged about your anger, you either think it is justified ('after what he or she did') or that everybody is getting at you ('poor me').

STOP COUNTER-COMPLAINING

When one partner brings up an issue but the other counters it with another problem, the situation can quickly degenerate into a row about dozens of issues with each one becoming harder to solve. Try this four-step plan:

1. **Break the connection between shame and blame.**
   - If you haven't started one already, keep an anger diary.
   - Write down the things that people say or do which trigger your shame. Compare what someone actually said against what you heard. Have you added extra interpretations? Is your reaction more about you than them?
   - What type of people trigger your shame-based anger? Are they in positions of authority, colleagues or somebody in a lower position? Sometimes, the people we meet today are standing in for someone from the past or allowing us to relive old patterns. For example, problems with authority figures could be about your parents or irritating colleagues could be replacing a bothersome brother or sister. When becoming angry with

shop assistants or subordinates at work, we are replaying how we were treated by our parents or teachers but compensating by taking the more powerful role.

- Understand how you convert shame to anger. Do you shout? Do you put people down? Do you nit-pick?

2. **Make a commitment to change.**
   - Double-check if someone really meant to shame you. In most cases, you will have overreacted.
   - Develop a new internal voice that counters the dark ones from the past. For example, when your employer stops by your desk, remind yourself: my boss is not my father. This will stop his comments being filtered through old scripts.
   - When you find yourself about to cross-complain, mentally pause and count to ten.

3. **Heal your shame.**
   - Build your self-respect on firmer founda-tions. This is a huge topic, so I have set aside a whole book in this series: *Learn to Love Yourself Enough*.

- However, rest assured, understanding the links between the past and today is half the journey to greater self-esteem.
- Learn to accept criticism as a gift. Someone has offered you a chance to grow or see yourself through their eyes. (Remember, you don't have to take everything on board – there might be some parts that you still feel are unjust but concentrate on the useful things you could adopt.)

4. **Treat others with respect.**
   - Instead of looking for things to criticise, start looking for things to praise.
   - Stop ignoring your partner when he or she has something to say – by walking away or burying yourself in a computer game or TV show – and start listening.
   - The better you treat your partner, the more respect they will have for you.

Paranoid Anger

These people are excessively suspicious. They are certain other people are trying to hurt them or do them down and therefore lower their guard. In the worst cases, they follow their partner around, cross-examine their movements, and search for proof of infidelity by monitoring texts and emails or listening in on phone calls. Although someone with paranoid anger will be anxious and upset most of the time, they do not generally express it. Unfortunately, this makes them quick to read anger in other people and to interpret their partner's behaviour and words in the worst possible light. I call this negative mind-reading.

When Zoë moved into Derek's flat she found a box of photographs recording all his golden moments with his ex-girlfriend. 'In my defence, they were on the bookcase – so it's not like I went hunting. I had a quick look when he was out and became transfixed by the sheer number. They couldn't have a glass of wine without a snapshot. I wouldn't mind, except he hardly ever takes a photo of us.' When she tackled Derek, he said he would put them up in the attic. This did not satisfy Zoë: 'If you really loved me, you would have destroyed them. I certainly haven't kept any old photographs of my boyfriends.' This is typical of negative mind-reading – there could be lots of innocent reasons why they were on his bookcase. 'To be honest, I'd forgotten all about them,' explained Derek. 'I don't really want to destroy them because they're a record of past holidays.' Zoë interpreted this as a sign that he was still in love with his previous girlfriend.

Like many people with paranoid anger, in the heat of the row, Zoë would react first and think second. This meant that she often went off at half-cock and ended up regretting a lot of what she said.

How to recognise it

While everyone can jump to the wrong conclusions, it turns into paranoid anger when:

- Instead of jealousy being a sign that something is wrong with a relationship – like an affair – it goes on for ever, whatever the explanation and reassurance from your partner.
- The feelings are very intense and people become more upset than the situation really merits.
- In the worst cases, it becomes obsessive and someone can think of very little else.

HOW TO KICK THE SURVEILLANCE HABIT

1. Accept that it is addictive and counter-productive.

2. If you are tempted, distract yourself for ten minutes by phoning a friend, reading the paper or fixing something nice for supper. In most cases, the urge will disappear.

3. What are you really trying to achieve? In most cases, a snooper wants reassurance. Instead of getting negative attention through a fight, ask for something positive like a cuddle.

4. If you tend to over-analyse every event, try writing down all your thoughts. Don't censor, get every-thing down on paper. Next, go through and cross off the exaggerations and strange leaps of logic. What is left? Normally, there are one or two small but manageable fears that need to be talked through with your partner.

5. Discuss what is acceptable access to each other's movements, data, private correspond-ence, and what is unreasonable.

Deliberate Anger

While the previous anger styles are driven by largely unconscious feelings, these people are only too aware of what they are doing and why. They come from angry families and learned from a young age that people who rant and rave often get their own way. Not only can someone with deliberate anger switch it on and off but they will often exaggerate to get their own way.

When I was a student, I lived in a block of flats that opened off a central staircase. One afternoon, returning back, I heard shouting and something being thrown above. When I reached the third landing, there was a woman picking up some broken crockery while her boyfriend fumed about her stupidity. Embarrassed, I looked the other way as I climbed past. However, the man stopped shouting, greeted me in a normal voice and tried both to normalise and make me complicit with a 'what can you do' shrug. By the time I reached my floor, he was screaming with rage again. He sounded out of control but, in reality, he could switch his anger off and on again.

An example of how deliberate anger is exaggerated comes from Emily, twenty-six. If her husband, Adam, was more than ten minutes late, she would fly into a rage, crying and accusing him of not loving her. 'If he truly loved me, he would know how important it is to me and not treat me so badly,' she explained. Later, in her counselling, Emily admitted that she did not always start off feeling angry. Sometimes she had been busy and not noticed the time. 'When I stopped and thought about it, I turned angrier and angrier: "How dare he? After everything I do for him."' Although Emily had deliberately switched on her anger, the burst of energy and the accompanying adrenaline rush had tipped her feelings from deliberate into real anger. In the worst cases, deliberate anger can become addictive.

How to recognise it

This kind of anger is about power and control and it is very common for both someone using deliberate anger and their partners to minimise the impact on their relationship and hope it will somehow get better. So be truthful when answering these questions. The first section is for someone using deliberate anger:

- Do you find it very hard to be vulnerable and let other people get too close for fear of being hurt?

- Do you use anger to avoid difficult and complicated feelings? By contrast, does anger feel pure and righteous?
- Is 'respect' more important to you than most people?
- Did you witness domestic violence as a child or were you physically abused yourself?
- Are there times when your partner is frightened and fears that you might harm him/her?
- In your heart of hearts, do you know that this behaviour is not acceptable and is incompatible with a happy relationship?

For the partners of someone using deliberate anger:

- Are you sometimes frightened of your partner and feel controlled?
- Does this somehow seem normal because your partner's behaviour corresponds to something you witnessed as a child?
- In a milder form, deliberate anger uses tears and 'poor me' behaviour to manipulate, but often it will involve abusive language, throwing things, shoving and slapping. This is domestic violence and is not acceptable.

For both of you:

If you recognise this behaviour in yourself or your partner, you should seek help from Relate (www.relate.org.uk) or Respect (www.respect.uk.net).

STOPPING USING DELIBERATE ANGER

At the milder end of this issue – where there is no violence – it is possible to break free on your own, but many people need professional help as well.

1. **Understand the pay-offs.** What are the benefits in the short term? What about the medium term? Are they outweighed by the problems in the long term?

2. **Make a commitment to change.** Write it down, as this will make your commitment more real, and sign it. Don't make the commitment on the back of a terrible argument, when you are trying to win back your partner, but as a calm, rational response to a pattern of behaviour that is not acceptable.

3. **Run your own life and let your partner run her or his life.** This will dramatically reduce the stress and reduce your anger. In the next

chapter, there are constructive ways – rather than bullying or nagging – to achieve change.

4. **If you need distance, ask for it.** Many people deliberately pick fights because they need time away. Break this habit by taking up a hobby that allows you time-out. For example, going fishing, walking a dog or going to the gym. If you know that a whole weekend together is too much, build in small blocks of time alone.

Moral Anger

One of the main problems with negative anger is that it builds and builds and arguments become more and more destructive. This next style is a sure sign that a couple have tipped from manageable – although still unpleasant – arguments into something nasty and toxic.

Someone with moral anger is always on the 'good side' of an argument. Their values are truths. When their partner disagrees, their points are not only dismissed but are also considered 'wrong', 'bad' or even 'evil' and their opinions are 'lies'. It goes without saying that someone with moral anger is judgmental and easily disappointed by other people. However, this is the most insidious twist, because their partner is so clearly wrong, they clearly 'deserve' to be punished, pulled down a peg, or belittled. The other partner fights back and this behaviour is used to justify another bout of moral anger.

When Gretchen couldn't stand yet another tirade from her husband, she walked out of the house. 'She left behind two small children,' complained Graham, 'she is clearly not a good mother.' With this black-and-white thinking, he dismissed Gretchen's views. 'I left them with their father and I only walked round the block to clear my head,' she explained. However, Graham used this incident to reduce the money he transferred each month to the household account. 'As she can't be trusted to put the interests of the children first, she can't be trusted with money.'

How to recognise it

Anger and moral certainty is a very dangerous combination. How many of the following statements about your partner do you agree with?

- I'm better than you.
- I know what's right better than you.

- I have better values than you.
- I'm right and you're wrong.

Even if you agreed with only one statement, this can be cause for alarm. However, the next two chapters will provide strategies for changing your thinking, learning to listen and improving communication with your partner. Meanwhile, the final exercise in this chapter will help you, whatever your anger style, to find a sense of proportion.

ANGER THERMOMETER

One of the problems with high-conflict relationships is that couples often overreact and become angrier than the offence demands. Therefore it helps to know, and name, all the gradations from calm up to apoplectic.

Everybody reacts differently and so everybody has a different range of feelings. I have put an example of an anger thermometer down the left-hand side and the right-hand side is blank for you. How would you describe your gradations? If you find anger difficult to express, you might like to add extra items at the bottom end of the scale. If you are too quick to express your anger, you might need more at the top end.

6. You let go of the anger once the problem is solved.

What to do about an angry partner

The main thrust of this chapter has been about helping people with their negative anger styles, but what if you are on the receiving end? It is easy to criticise our partner and overlook our own contribution. Remembering that most issues are 'six of one and half a dozen of the other' (see Chapter One), could you be unwittingly encouraging your partner to become angrier and to turn healthy anger into one of the negative anger styles? Once your partner has cooled down, do you discuss and address the issues or do you keep quiet for fear of more arguments? Nothing is solved by avoiding conflict, and more anger is stored away for next time round.

When there is another angry outburst, don't lose your temper too – but try and react with calmness, hear him or her out, and respond with moderation (challenge any 'all or nothing' thinking). If your partner gets so angry that these tactics fail, it is probably because she or he has reached fever pitch. In the same way that there is no point reasoning with a drunk, it is counter-productive to argue with someone who has gone ballistic. When your partner is rational again, explain how his or her anger impacts on you. If he or she brushes off your concerns or rationalises the problem away, stick to your guns and explain in further detail the effect on the family and how anger is making it harder to resolve your differences.

Finally, adopt a positive attitude to anger yourself and learn the constructive ways to communicate in the next chapter. Little changes in your behaviour can have a big knock-on effect on your relationship.

Summing Up

Although anger can be positive, it makes us uncomfortable and many people suppress their feelings. Unfortunately, the anger is still there and bursts out in one or more of the six negative forms. However, by slowing down our automatic reactions, understanding what triggers rows and learning to express emotions in an appropriate manner, negative anger can be transformed into healthy anger.

IN A NUTSHELL:

- Accept anger as a normal part of life and of being human.
- If your rows become about how you argue and what was said, rather than solving the original trigger, this is a sign of negative anger styles.
- Improving how you handle anger will provide a positive role model for your partner and dramatically improve your communication.

STEP 4

DEVELOP YOUR ASSERTIVENESS

The goal of this book is to develop open and honest communication, so that you and your partner cooperate to resolve your differences. In step one, you took stock of your relationship (and began to identify some of the underlying problems). In step two, you learned that avoiding arguments stores up problems for the future. Step three dealt with anger. In this next part of the book, we come to the heart of problem-solving. Unfortunately, we are not born with the necessary skills for open and honest communication. It's not until we are about five or six that we develop the ability to think through a problem, consider the opinions and feelings of others and learn enough language to negotiate. Up to this point, a small child has two options. The first is to be a people-pleaser and go along with what Mummy or Daddy want

– which guarantees our parents' love but does not necessarily mean that we get what we want. The second is to become aggressive and demanding (this can involve temper tantrums, tears, wheedling, sulking and grabbing). It is very effective for getting what we want, but puts up a barrier between us and everybody else.

The children who adopt the people-pleasing option can grow up to be adults who will do anything for a quiet life (and fall into the low-conflict trap). The children who adopt the aggressive or demanding style tend to grow into adults who want to win at any price (and fall into the high-conflict trap). Fortunately, there is an alternative: becoming assertive.

Assertiveness training has got a bad name – because many people confuse it with being aggressive. In reality, it goes to the heart of open and honest communication. It is about stating our needs and goals (rather than hiding them behind people-pleasing) but being equally aware and respectful of other people's needs and goals (rather than steamrollering over them). Most assertiveness training will start with a list of basic rights but they boil down to just three key ones. The good courses will also cover how these rights are balanced by those of our partners:

My Rights	**My Partner's Rights**
To ask for what I want	To refuse your request
To be listened to and taken seriously	To be listened to and taken seriously
To be myself and have space/time to develop as an individual	To rely on you for love, support and consideration

Remember that there are always two sides to assertiveness training: respecting your partner's rights but, at the same time, not neglecting your own.

LOOKING THROUGH ASSERTIVE EYES

Before working on your own behaviour, it is always easier to spot overly aggressive or people-pleasing behaviour in other people.

Start by looking at work colleagues and friends. How do they react if someone makes an impossible demand? Do they agree and get stressed from all the extra work? (People-pleasing.) Maybe they fly off the handle? (Aggressive.) Perhaps they are accommodating to the person making the demand but take out their frustration on other colleagues? (Combination of people-pleasing and aggressive.) Hopefully, your colleague will explain their other commitments and negotiate another solution for getting the work done. (Assertive.)

Turning to home life, how do your partner or your children react to a request? What triggers an aggressive or people-pleasing response? In contrast, what triggers an assertive one? Look closely at the differences that generate the positive outcome. What sort of language is used? What about body language and tone of voice?

Finally, start observing yourself. How do you respond to authority figures – like your doctor, your children's teachers or the woman taking your yoga class – who say something with which you disagree? Is your natural response to nod and accept it – but inwardly fume? When a sales assistant is rude or annoyed that your perfectly reasonable request is causing extra work, do you become angry and aggressive? In contrast, how do you feel when you speak your mind but keep your temper under control – so that your reaction is in proportion to the offence?

How Your Body Language Gives You Away

When couples in counselling report back on an argument during the week, they are often surprised at how some relatively innocent remark sparked a huge row. However, the problem is not so much what was said, but the manner in which it was expressed. This is because our true feelings leak out through our body language:

Aggressive body language

This is shown in the following ways:

- **Posture:** Hands on the hips with elbows pointing out. Aggressive people pull themselves up to their full height to look as tall and dominant as possible.
- **Facial muscles:** A tight, taught look around the face. Gritted teeth. Eyes narrowed. Any smile does not reach the eyes.
- **Movements:** Tense and jerky. Impatience is shown by rubbing hands or tapping feet. Aggressive people will stand too close.
- **Gestures:** Finger wagging or clenched fists. Patronising touching or patting on the shoulder. Short quick nods to say 'get on with it'.

- **Eye contact:** Staring. No blinking.
- **Tone:** Louder, harsher than usual. By contrast, some people are threateningly quiet.

People-pleasing body language

The following signs should be easy to spot:

- **Posture:** Round-shouldered – as if someone is trying to look smaller and less significant. Crossed arms – as if they are protecting or hugging themselves. When seated, someone with passive body language will almost curl in on themselves.
- **Facial muscles:** A gloomy, over-apologetic, pleading look. Chewing lower lip. Chin dropped towards the chest.
- **Movements:** Tense, agitated, fidgeting. People-pleasers will often become clumsy and start dropping things. They will also back away and leave too much distance between themselves and the person speaking.
- **Gestures:** Fiddling with clothes, hair or pens. The hand covers the mouth and there is lots of face-touching. Alternatively, there are few movements or gestures – like someone is trying to be invisible. This is normally a sign of low self-esteem.

- **Eye contact:** People-pleasers find it hard to make eye contact. Either the eyes are lowered or they dart nervously around. Another strategy is to close the eyes for long stretches of time – as if, like an ostrich burying its head in the sand, what they can't see won't hurt them. Alternatively, someone who people-pleases will hang on every word.
- **Tone:** Quiet. The speech is tentative or mumbling. There is also an apologetic or whining note in the voice.

Assertive body language

By contrast, these messages are much more neutral:

- **Posture:** Open. Hands hang loosely by the side or are placed in the lap. Little crossing of arms and legs.
- **Facial muscles:** Relaxed and sincere with plenty of smiles.
- **Movements:** Steady, fluid and regular. Someone with assertive body language will lean forward to the person speaking – to show interest. Their head is erect in a responsive rather than threatening way.

- **Gestures:** These will match what is being said. There are no intrusive or excessive mannerisms.
- **Eye contact:** Good. Small nods show that the person talking is being heard and encouraged to say more.
- **Tone:** Evenly pitched, steady and easily heard.

IMPROVE YOUR BODY LANGUAGE

Draining excess aggression or submission out of your body will improve your partner's reactions and reduce miscommunication, and changing your outward posture will also change how you feel inside.

1. **Dealing with anger:** Starting with your toes and feet and moving up your buttocks, fists, shoulders and face, clench everything. Hold for a second or two. Then, slowly, release all the tension from your muscles. Shake it out and go as limp as the surroundings allow. Finally take one or two deep breaths.

2. **Go to a beautiful place:** We all have favourite spots. It could be your garden, a stunning view or a calmness that comes from sustained exercise such as swimming or jogging. Where

is your beautiful place? Close your eyes and really make the picture come to life. What details are particularly pleasing? What about the smells? What can you hear? Next time you feel overwhelmed or frightened by the world, superimpose this positive picture over the negative one.

3. **Become more positive:** Adopt an assertive body language. Imagine an upside-down triangle across your partner's eyebrows and nose and keep your eyes fixed on this zone. Sit or lean forward, so that you can monitor your partner's response and gauge the effect of your message. Don't hide behind a newspaper or ask for something you'd like from another room. If you are relaxed and open, your partner will subconsciously match your assertive manner.

Assertiveness in Action

There are two elements to assertive communication: *good body language*, which we have already covered, and *building agreement*. The following case history illuminates this second point.

Philip and Sophie were both in their early forties and had first met at school. Over the years, Philip's confidence grew as his business took off and made more and more money. This had allowed Sophie to give up her job and concentrate on bringing up their two children. Although she had no regrets about this decision, her confidence and self-esteem went in the opposite direction to Philip's. The couple arrived for their weekly counselling session with thunderous faces. Sophie had spent a lot of time arranging a family barbecue and party: 'I'd bought some lights to hang round the pool and spent hours making the garden look special. It had been a long time since we'd had both our families over and I was looking forward to a great weekend. Two days before the party, Philip dropped a bombshell: he'd invited two business colleagues along.'

Although Sophie was furious on the inside, she basically kept quiet: 'I didn't want a scene or to spoil the party,' she said. This is typical people-pleasing behaviour. In contrast, Philip was aggressive (the two behaviours often go hand in hand). 'You should have known that they were only in the UK for a few days and I would have to entertain them,' he said. 'Anyway, why on earth did we spend all that money on the garden and pool if it wasn't going to help the business?' This blaming and judgmental language is a hallmark of aggression. He also upped the stakes with inflammatory remarks: 'You don't understand anything' and 'If you'd just listen for a change'.

Unfortunately, the party had been a disaster; the family did not really have anything to say to the business contacts and tended to talk to each other. Philip thought: 'Your family were rude and made guests in my house feel ostracised.' Worse still, the boys had started dive-bombing the pool and had soaked one of the businessmen.

Instead of standing up for herself and perhaps saying that it had been a mistake to mix two very different sets of people – which would have been assertive – Sophie had used people-pleasing techniques and tried to diffuse Philip's anger with excessive explanation and excuses: 'I was having trouble because the hollandaise sauce was curdling. I probably let the bowl get too warm. My sister was telling me a long story about her move, so I couldn't be watching the children.' She was also offering lots of justification: 'It's been ages since the family has got together and there was lots of news to catch up on' and 'The boys had been cooped up revising for their exams and they needed to let off steam.'

Her final signature people-pleasing behaviour was over-apologising: 'As I've said a hundred times, it won't happen again. I've spoken to my sister and she's disciplined her son.' Unfortunately, this just made Philip see red: 'Can't you even do this one thing right?' Criticism without offering a solution is typical aggressive behaviour.

Instead of letting this argument go round and round in circles, getting nastier and nastier, I took them through the six ingredients for an assertive discussion where both sides have the right to ask for what they want, to be listened to and taken seriously and, where it is possible, to refuse a request:

Support each other's position

Sophie said: 'I understand that it would be rude to dump them in a strange town over the weekend.' Philip said: 'I accept that we don't get much time as a family – all together.'

Offer praise

Sophie said: 'You work really hard and I don't tell you enough how proud I am of all you've achieved.' Philip said: 'You had the garden looking really nice.'

Build bridges

Philip said: 'I would have preferred it if everybody had mixed.' Sophie said: 'If I'd had more notice, I could have hired some help so that I wouldn't have spent so much time in the kitchen.'

Allow for alternative viewpoints

Sophie said: 'I realise that work comes first for you – after all, it pays for everything – but I think you need to relax more.' Philip said: 'I know that you're not really interested in the money markets and I realise that, to outsiders, it can easily get technical.'

Allow for the fact that you may be wrong

Philip said: 'Perhaps I was asking too much.' Sophie said: 'I could have made more of an effort.'

Look for a compromise

Sophie said: 'Perhaps we could have had them over to the house another time.' Philip said: 'Perhaps I could have booked them theatre tickets instead and I could have enjoyed the family more.'

ASSERTIVENESS QUIZ

Look at the following five scenarios and pick out the people-pleasing, the aggressive and, finally, the assertive response.

1. Your partner accepts an invitation to the party of a couple whom you dislike. What is your reaction?
    a) List all the other times that she or he did not consult you;
    b) Suddenly remember something urgent at work that stops you attending;
    c) Listen to your partner's explanation, explain your misgivings, and agree to put in a quick appearance but not stay late.

2. Your partner is hanging over your shoulder, trying to attract your attention, while you are doing something that needs complete concentration. Do you . . .
    a) Ask if you could talk later;
    b) Tell him or her to back off;
    c) Stop and talk, as it must be important?

3. You need time off work for something important but your supervisor says all the spaces on the holiday rota are taken. What do you do?

a) Go over your supervisor's head;
b) Clarify why it is important and ask for your supervisor's help in finding a way round the problem;
c) Phone in sick on that day.

4. Your partner wants to try something a little spicy in the bedroom. What's your reaction?
a) Use the request as an opportunity to re-evaluate your love life;
b) Accuse him or her of having an affair;
c) Feel guilty that you're not good enough and reluctantly go along with it.

5. Your partner is sulking or angry and complains: 'You never do anything I want.' Which is most likely to be your reply?
a) 'I'm sorry, but I do my best.'
b) 'Have you ever stopped to think why?'
c) '*Never* is putting it a bit strongly.'

Congratulate yourself if you spotted the following:
Aggressive – 1a, 2b, 3a, 4b, 5b.
People-pleasing – 1b, 2c, 3c, 4c, 5a.
Assertive – 1c, 2a, 3b, 4a, 5c.

Now go back over the questions and think which answer you would have given in each scenario.

The Right to Say No

Returning to the basic rights described at the beginning of the chapter, how do you reconcile your right to ask with your partner's right to refuse? First, you need to check that you are asking: 'Would you . . .?' or 'Could you . . .?' rather than giving an order: 'Don't leave your clothes on the floor' or 'Empty the washing machine'. Next, make certain your partner has all the relevant information to fully assess your request. For example: 'I am going to be home late, so would you mind . . .?' These two strategies will significantly increase the chance of getting a 'yes'.

What if you need to say 'no' to your partner? Remember, you always have the right to refuse and it is often better to know that something is not possible – and make alternative arrangements – than be let down. More importantly, you are refusing the request, not the person. Next, use the ABC of communication:

A is for address the question: *I can't pick you up from work*

B is for bridge: *but, however, unfortunately, because*

C is for communicate: *the car is going to be in the garage*

Finally, offer an alternative workable compromise. *'Why don't we come home on the train together?'* or *'If you stay later at work, I could collect you when the car's ready.'* If you and your partner still cannot agree, there is more advice in another book in the Seven Steps series: *Help Your Partner Say 'Yes'*.

Summing Up

We are not born assertive; it takes time to develop the ability to think through a problem and understand someone else's point of view. When we are under stress, we tend to act on gut reaction (learned as small children) rather than access our adult skills: explaining how we feel and think, in a direct, honest, appropriate and spontaneous way. The good news is that these skills become easier with practice.

IN A NUTSHELL:

- Think of your other half as a partner for problem solving, not an opponent.
- What are the similarities, differences and where do your goals dovetail? Look for a solution that is win/win.
- Never forget you and your partner have equal rights.

5

HOW TO ARGUE
EFFECTIVELY

The assertive skills outlined in the last chapter assume that both parties can remain calm and rational. This is easier with work colleagues or friends whose behaviour may hurt but seldom devastates us. When it comes to our partners, we might be assertive about minor matters – such as who's picking up the children – but what about the big issues? And what if we have fundamentally opposing opinions? In these circumstances, it is highly likely that the two of you will row. Remember, there is nothing wrong with a *good* argument. This is where both sides passionately hold an opinion, express it with consideration for the other person, listen to the opposing view, look for a solution and make up afterwards. What you don't want is a *bad* argument. This will involve name-calling, trying to win at all costs (even if it includes destroying your partner), not listening or walking away in the middle of a row, no solution and a lingering, nasty atmosphere. Although sometimes people think they have bad rows because their partner is a bad person, in my experience it is nearly always because someone is scared (so runs away or lashes out) or, more likely, does not know how to argue successfully.

Three Steps to Conflict Resolution

1. Explore: 'I need to say . . .'

This is all about venting anger, explaining griev- ances and frustrations. Sometimes, one partner will need to do more venting. Don't try and reason; someone gripped by emotions will not have access to their rational mind. However, acknowledge their feelings: 'I can see you are upset.' Make certain all the feelings have been vented before moving on to the second step. Check with each other: do you need to say anything more?

Breakthrough tip: Don't get personal. Rather than criticising the person, complain about the behaviour. Instead of 'You're so untidy' try 'Please do not leave your coffee cup on the side.'

2. Comprehending

Really hear each other out. Don't use the time when your partner is talking to rehearse your defence – listen. Ask questions, so that you are clear what is meant and make certain that there are no misunderstandings. If you pay your partner the compliment of active listening, they will return the favour. If you are unable to listen, it probably means that you are still angry and need to vent some more.

Part one: What is my responsibility?
Remembering that rows are 'six of one and half a dozen of the other', think about your contribution. How has your behaviour extended or deepened the problem? When you have a clear idea of your own failings, find something – however small – and apologise for it.

For example, Nick and Anna, from Chapter Two, fought after their son's poor mock GCSE results. Anna had been away on a training course and blamed Nick for not supervising his revision properly in her absence. The row went round and round in circles. Anna still felt annoyed, but apologised for her contribution to the friction: 'I'm sorry that I gave you the silent treatment.' A few hours later, and after much reflection, Anna had another apology: 'I was angry with our son, and I'm sorry I took some of it out on you.'

Breakthrough tip: Good questions start with 'who', 'what', 'when', 'where', but be careful with 'why'. These questions can sometimes sound like accusations rather than invitations to talk – so try softening the effect with 'Have you any idea . . .' (why you feel angry) or 'Could you explain . . .' (why you walked away).

Part two: I comprehend your problems

Try and look at matters from your partner's viewpoint. Are there any mitigating circumstances? What problems could he or she have been facing at the time? Is there anything from their past that makes this a blind spot? For example, Anna told Nick: 'It must have been hard taking on both parental roles while I was away.'

Breakthrough tip: Sometimes when couples find it difficult to apologise for their contribution or find any mitigation for their partner, I ask them to change seats and literally imagine themselves in their partner's shoes. Five minutes arguing the other side is normally enough, but it is also an effective trick for understanding your partner's case better. Some couples change chairs at home; some cross over and argue from different corners of the room and some make the switch just in their head. If you find it impossible to step into your partner's shoes, you are probably still too angry. In this case, return to exploring.

3. Action

Until you have both vented your feelings and both tried to comprehend each other's viewpoint, it is impossible to find a solution that will stick. Unfortunately, some couples try and move straight to action. As previously discussed, these short-cut solutions can work but generally leave one partner feeling resentful and therefore sow the seeds for future disputes.

When Nick and Anna truly understood each other's side of the row, Nick agreed to make supervising their son's schoolwork a greater priority, while Anna agreed that next time work took her away she'd try and get ahead of the laundry so that Nick had more time to devote to their son.

Ask yourself: 'What have we learned from this fight?' 'Would we do anything different if these circumstances came up again?' 'How will we do things differently next time?' 'What should we do about this problem now?'

Breakthrough tip: Don't be obsessed with winning. Either try to find a compromise, which pleases both parties, or aim for a trade-off: 'I won't read in bed if you give up the horrible habit of dunking biscuits in your tea.' However, being aware of the sensitive areas, and agreeing to tread lightly, is often enough of an outcome.

WORKING THROUGH THE THREE STEPS TO CONFLICT RESOLUTION

Many couples either want to minimise disagreements or get over them as quickly as possible. Therefore, this exercise is designed to slow down your journey through the three steps.

1. Take three pieces of paper and mark one of them EXPLORE, another COMPREHEND and the third one ACTION.

2. Take either a current dispute or an argument that you had recently.

3. Exploring is all about feelings – so each time one of you comes up with a feeling write it down on the EXPLORE page.

4. Exploring is also about opinions and beliefs: 'A good father would look after his kids; a good wife would not go out in the evening.' Write all this down too.

5. Exploring is about facts: 'I can't get home before seven fifteen', 'Our household generates ten loads of washing a week and someone needs to do it.' Write the most important ones down.

6. Check back over your EXPLORE page. Make certain that along with the facts there are plenty of feeling words and beliefs. Can you think of anything more from either of these two categories?

7. Sometimes a potential solution (for the ACTION sheet) might come up early in the conversation. Write the discovery on the relevant sheet, so it's not lost, but return to filling up the EXPLORE sheet.

8. Next take the COMPREHEND sheet. Comprehending is about why things happen. For example: 'I get angry because I'm stressed from work' or 'I don't feel like sex when I'm ignored.' Write these down.

9. Beliefs always come from somewhere: our upbringing, religion, general culture or the media. The particularly powerful ones are from our childhood. How might your upbringing affect your beliefs? Write down your findings.

10. Looking at the EXPLORE and COMPREHEND pages. How can you use these insights to find a solution?

11. Solutions work best when there is a benefit for each party. For example, Partner A agrees to give Partner B five minutes' peace and quiet after arriving home, but, in exchange, Partner B agrees to give the children a bath later in the evening so that A can rest. Make the tasks something that can be checked – as above – rather than general and hard to verify, such as 'to try harder'. Write the agreement on the ACTION page. You could even write it like a contract: 'I agree to . . . if you agree to . . .' and both sign it.

12. A week later bring out the ACTION sheet and see if both of you have kept your side of the bargain. If you haven't, take three new pieces of paper, write out the headings, and go through the exercise again, exploring how both of you feel, comprehending what went wrong and setting a better action plan.

What Type of Listener are You?

There are two halves of an effective argument. The first is obvious: communicating our feelings, beliefs and opinions. Sometimes, we think that if only we can properly explain our viewpoint everything will be fine. However, many people overlook the second half of the equation. Unless we are a good listener, we will not understand our partner's viewpoint and, worse still, he or she will become more and more frustrated and less able to hear us. The result is a downward spiral of misinformation, misunderstanding and misery.

There are three kinds of listening – argumentative, dismissive or respectful – and although we can switch between them during an argument, most us of have a core style.

Argumentative

While one partner is talking, the other is waiting to jump in, correct or disagree. The result is a lot of interruptions and the main issue can easily be lost in a maze of side arguments.

Amelia and Howard, both in their mid-thirties, had financial problems but, rather than discussing how to solve them, they would fight about particular purchases. 'The flat-screen TV was a bargain, it was too good to miss and, anyway, it will encourage us to stay in more and spend less,' explained Howard. 'Except it wasn't a good deal, was it?' Amelia interrupted. She had found the real price that he had paid from his online account. 'I also looked at several price comparison sites and you were done.' Howard fought back by itemising the cost of Amelia's recent meals out with the girls.

In my experience, arguments about facts get couples nowhere. First, this is because 'facts' are always open to different interpretation. Second, facts suggest right and wrong, a winner and a loser. Howard and Amelia were soon fighting about who was under the most stress and who contributed more to their marriage. However, they needed to work together if they were ever to solve their problems.

Dismissive

Although the previous listening style is destructive, at least everything is out in the open. This second style is more internal and therefore harder to recognise. While one partner is talking, the other is putting mental brackets round some parts of the argument. This bracketing allows the listener to first play down the importance of the disputed sentence and then dismiss it altogether.

Jacob and Stephanie had been married for seven years and had a three-year-old child. They had a terrible fight after Stephanie had phoned and asked Jacob to pick up some essential groceries on his way home and he had forgotten to. 'We live miles from the nearest shop and it's a real trek on the bus,' Stephanie explained. 'I'd meant to get them. I had the best of intentions but my mind was too full of work,' countered Jacob. When we deconstructed their argument, we found two rounds of bracketing. First, for Jacob, his good intentions allowed him to bracket Stephanie's frustration as unreasonable: 'I really meant to go.' For him, therefore, her anger was out of all proportion to the offence and he dismissed it. Meanwhile, Stephanie bracketed all Jacob's worry about a complex law case that he was wrapped up in: 'He's always stressed by work, so there was nothing new.' This allowed her to dismiss his mitigating circumstances.

The second round of dismissive listening came later that night. Jacob stormed out of the house and drove to the supermarket. When Stephanie tried to explain why she was so upset, Jacob closed down the conversation: 'You've got your things. End of argument.' He sighed and looked at me for support: 'She got what she wanted and she's still angry.' Stephanie turned to me: 'I'm still angry because he just walked away mid-argument.' This is the cruellest form of dismissive listening.

Respectful

When scientists watch newly wed couples argue, they can predict with 94 per cent accuracy which couples will stay married and which will divorce. In some cases, they only need to listen for a few minutes. The key ingredient for a successful marriage is respectful listening. So I helped Stephanie and Jacob replay their argument and asked them to add as many respectful and supportive comments as they could from the list below:

'You've got a good point.'
'Yes, I see.'
'So what you're saying is . . .'
'I can see how you feel.'
'Right.'
'Go on.'
'Tell me more.'
'I agree.'
'OK, so what do you suggest?'
'What do you think?'
'How do you feel?'

These phrases show that although you might disagree, you are prepared to respect your partner's right to hold a different viewpoint. They are also a constant reminder that you might be arguing, but that you will survive, find a solution and put it behind you. In addition, they lower the tension and stop the argument getting out of hand. So how did Stephanie and Jacob's argument replay with respectful listening?

'I was really angry that you forgot the groceries,' said Stephanie.
'*Go on*,' replied Jacob.
'Our daughter was refusing to get into the bath.'

'*So what you're saying is* that you were at the
end of your tether.'

'I don't feel that I get enough support.'

'I want to support you but you get so angry.'

'*You've got a good point,*' replied Stephanie. 'It
must drive people away.'

'But *I can see how you feel* because I was angry
at myself too. I really wanted to help but I
let myself down.'

Although stopping to look at my flip-chart of
respectful phrases felt a bit contrived, Stephanie
and Jacob discovered more about each other than
before and, more importantly, laid the founda-
tions for a solution. Even better, after a couple of
weeks, respectful listening became second nature
and they found their own vocabulary.

IMPROVE YOUR COMMUNICATION

This is a fun game to play with your partner but it
has a serious intention and will reveal a lot about
how the two of you communicate.

- Sitting back to back, the first partner makes a
  simple line drawing – like the one on the page
  opposite.

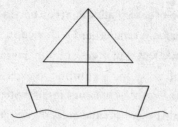

- The first partner does not show the second partner the picture but has to give instructions, so that the second partner can draw it. For example, 'Start at the top of the page, in the middle, and draw a straight line halfway down.' You *can't* describe the picture – 'draw a flower' – but you *can* use geometric terms like 'draw a circle'.

- The second partner can ask questions and check that they have heard the instructions correctly.

- Take as long as you like. It's not a race. Don't worry about being a good artist. This exercise is about communication.

- Keep your instructions short and to the point. Too much information, too quickly, will lead to confusion.

- When you have finished, show each other your pictures and post-mortem what helped make the picture an accurate copy and what hindered.

- Swap over so that both of you have a chance to describe a picture and a chance to follow the instructions and draw.

This is an exercise that I use in my workshops and it is interesting what people learn. Some 'drawers' don't ask many questions and just assume that they are right. Some 'drawers' are impatient and want to get on with the task and therefore miss vital information. Successful 'drawers' keep checking that they have heard correctly: 'Did you say a forty-five-degree angle?' Some 'describers' leave out vital bits of information, give contradictory instructions or don't check that their partner has heard properly. What everybody learns is just how much time it takes to communicate effectively.

Four Personal Philosophies for Effective Arguments

So far in this chapter, we have looked at the shape of good argument and the importance of truly listening. The final ingredient is the right frame of mind.

Look for the good in the other person

Sometimes my female clients claim that their husbands are so bad at communicating feelings, and anger in particular, that it is impossible to argue effectively. I tend to shy away from gender stereotypes, partly because I have met plenty of emotionally articulate men and women who are not 'in touch with their feelings' but mainly because of the 'six of one and half a dozen of the other' rule (see Chapter One). Nearly every woman who complains about her partner using one of the anger avoidance strategies turns out to be using a complementary one herself. Sometimes it is easier to criticise our partner rather than to understand our own contribution. This is why it is important to look for the good in your partner. If this feels difficult, try and understand how your partner arrived at his or her viewpoint. Eventually, you will move away from holding black-and-white positions and become aware of the grey in between.

Be flexible

Accept that there is no absolute truth about anything – only our own personal truths. Therefore, we should allow our partners to have a different view of our relationship – and not feel too challenged by it. After all, your partner is living with you, which is one experience; and you living with him or her is another experience. To explore the idea of being more flexible, make a list of all the things you *need* from a relationship (like trust, honesty, companionship) and all the things you would *like*. How many things on the 'need' list are truly needs rather than preferences? Could something be transferred to the wish list? Finally, ask yourself: Am I asking too much from my partner? Could someone like a friend or even a professional provide this role? For example, some partners find it hard to sit with pain or grief. It might be desirable for your partner to be supportive and listen to complaints about your difficult mother or how much you miss your deceased father – but it might be asking too much.

Be optimistic

Optimistic people believe that there will be a good outcome from an argument. They will learn something important and find a resolution to a sticky problem. This allows them to avoid hopeless comments which can turn a manageable row into a potential tragedy: 'We'll never sort this out' or 'If you feel like that, I can't see the point in carrying on.' Better still, optimistic people put the problem down to something specific and transitory – 'we've both been stressed lately' – and therefore feel better able to cope and to search for a solution. By contrast, pessimists put problems down to something general and ingrained – 'We're incompatible' – and therefore feel hopeless and overwhelmed. For help becoming more optimistic, see the final philosophy and the exercise at the end of this section.

Accentuate the positive

Generally it is easier to say what we don't want than to ask for what we do want. That's why, when trying to make things better with our partners, we end up either complaining or simply describing the problem.

So, thinking of your complaints about your partner, write down the top three and turn them into positive requests: what you want rather than what you don't want. The more specific you can be the better.

For example:
Complaint: *You sulk to get your own way.*
Positive request: *Please tell me outright when you disagree.*

How will I know when this has been achieved?:
When we can happily go shopping together.

Concrete goal: *Let's choose the new taps for the kitchen together.*

Complaint: *I'm always the driving force.*

Positive request: *Don't leave all the decisions to me.*

How will I know when this has been achieved?:
When my partner arranges a night out.

Concrete goal: *Actively planning a holiday together.*

EXERCISE: ACCENTUATE THE POSITIVE

Look at these typical complaints and see if you could turn them into a positive and then find a request for a concrete but small goal. (Some possible answers can be found below.)

1. Why do I always have to clear up?
2. Will you stop mauling me?
3. You never initiate sex.
4. You're always hanging out with your friends.
5. I hate it when you avoid me.
6. You are way too critical.
7. Why can't you lighten up?
8. Why didn't you phone me?

9. You do nothing with the kids.
10. Isn't it about time you fixed the hall light?

1. Why do I always have to clear up?
Positive: I'm really grateful when you help me keep the house clean.
Concrete goal: It would mean a lot to me if you emptied the bin.

2. Will you stop mauling me?
Positive: I like it when you stroke me gently.
Concrete goal: Would you give me a soothing back massage?

3. You never initiate sex.
Positive: I loved it that time that you seduced me.
Concrete goal: I'm going to back off asking and wait until you feel ready.

4. You're always hanging out with your friends.
Positive: I love our time together.
Concrete goal: Shall we go to the movies on Wednesday?

5. I hate it when you avoid me.
Positive: It's great when you get home early.

Concrete goal: Let's meet up after work and go for a drink together.

6. You are way too critical.
   Positive: I really appreciated it when you complimented me about . . .
   Concrete goal: I think we should try and say thank you to each other more often.

7. Why can't you lighten up?
   Positive: I really enjoy our fun times together.
   Concrete goal: Let's do something great this weekend.

8. Why didn't you phone me?
   Positive: It's so nice to hear your voice during the day.
   Concrete goal: Let's try and touch base with each other sometime tomorrow.

9. You do nothing with the kids.
   Positive: It means so much to the kids when you do things with them.
   Concrete goal: Could you take the kids to the park this afternoon?

10. Isn't it about time you fixed the hall light?

Positive: Thank you so much for fixing the sticky drawer, it's made my life so much easier.

Concrete goal: Do you think you'll be able to fix the hall light this weekend?

What if the Argument Turns Destructive?

Even with the best will in the world, sometimes a productive argument can go off the rails, but don't panic. Remember, it is better to have a bad argument than none at all.

- When the temperature rises, this is usually a sign that the real feelings are beginning to come to the surface and a sign of hope. In counselling, the arguments get worse before they get better.

- Resist the temptation to say 'and another thing' and throw in additional gripes. These examples might strengthen your case, but they also prolong and complicate the argument. Instead, try to solve one issue at a time.

- Have you been criticising rather than complaining? In general, complaints use 'I' while criticism uses 'You'. For example, a complaint would be: 'I wanted us to go to bed at the same time.' While a criticism would be: 'You didn't come to bed on time.' The first invites a discussion about bedtimes, the second will make your partner defensive and prolong an argument.

- Shouting and getting passionate are acceptable. But if the language gets abusive or there is even a threat of pushing or slapping, you should separate for ten to fifteen minutes and return when both of you have cooled down. Whoever feels threatened should call time-out. This means separating to different rooms or allowing one another to go out for a short walk/drive. The exact length of time apart is up to each couple but should be negotiated beforehand. It is vital that discussion is resumed – some couples have a quick post-mortem and others enter round two – otherwise the person in the middle of venting their feelings will be unwilling to let their partner have time-out for fear of not getting an opportunity to properly release.

- Remember the eighty/twenty rule (Chapter One) and look at what might be lying underneath the arguments that keep returning and returning and returning. One couple, in counselling, fought about defrosting the freezer. She felt that he bought too many frozen products without using up what was already there. He did the cooking and felt it was up to him to plan the meals. It got very nasty, especially as her parents had given them lots of chicken, which he claimed took up most of the space. This battle kept on recurring, with variations, for several weeks and still the freezer had not been defrosted. Finally, we looked deeper and found the core issue. The wife had bought the freezer before he moved in, and felt that he did not respect her property. In her opinion, if the freezer was not properly maintained it would break down and they couldn't afford a new one. Her husband had a more 'come what may' approach to money and generally felt that they would muddle through. When he truly understood his partner's fears, the issue disappeared and the freezer was finally defrosted.

- Use the Three Steps to Conflict Resolution exercise (see page 132) to post-mortem your argument. A good opening gambit would be to apologise for your half of the argument. Next look at what went wrong. A good way to achieve this, without reigniting the row, would be to say something like: 'I don't want to bring up the issues again, but why do you think it got out of hand?' 'How could we have approached it differently?' 'What can we learn?'

Summing Up

If arguments go round in circles, it is often because one of the three stages of conflict resolution – explore, comprehend, action – has been skipped. Arguing and properly making up again is the most intense form of bonding you can have. Isn't it about time to prove how much you love your partner by having a really good argument?

IN A NUTSHELL:

- Express yourself in simple and short sentences, and concentrate on one idea at a time. Your partner will only be able to absorb so much information.
- Better communication starts with better listening. You do not have to agree with your partner but at least look at the situation through their eyes and understand.
- Think about how you can turn your complaints into positive requests.

STEP 6

SAVING THE
SITUATION

In most cases, it is not so important *what* you are arguing about but *how*. Good technique and consideration will triumph over most problems. However, there are some situations which merit special discussion. This chapter is devoted to those topics where extra information or a different approach is necessary to resolve your differences.

Money Issues

Financial problems are always difficult to discuss, partly because money worries permeate every corner of a couple's life, but mainly because arguments are always about more than costs, spending priorities and overdrafts.

Louise and Will, both in their mid-thirties, got into trouble when Louise's maternity benefits ended. 'We used to have plenty of money, foreign holidays and time together,' explains Louise, 'but now we hardly see each other and when we do, we end up rowing about money. Yet the worst part is that I feel so helpless.'

While Louise became a worrier, Will tried to cope with the crisis by switching off. 'I'm under a lot of pressure at work, so I need to relax at home or my head will explode,' he explains. 'I'll play games on the computer or go off fishing at the weekend. OK, we've money problems, but what's the point of obsessing?'

Like most couples with financial problems, they are on a money see-saw. So that the more one partner pushes down on their end, the higher up (and more extreme) the other goes. In the case of Louise and Will, the more 'unconcerned' – at least on the surface – that he became, the more 'worried' she became. It had got to the point where they found it impossible to discuss their finances as even the slightest disagreement could turn nasty.

Nowhere is the money see-saw more marked than when couples become 'saver' and 'spender'. Jake and Carol had been married for almost twenty years but had never really sorted their finances out. Jake believed that Carol's spending was out of control. 'She's always coming back from the shops with piles of bags,' he complained. 'It's not like they're all for me,' she countered. 'I used to buy him something nice, like a jumper, but he'd get so upset that I stopped.' Unfortunately, whenever Jake got angry – normally after discovering Carol had taken out another loan – she got depressed and felt the need to raise her mood with another shopping trip. Their problems were made worse because they had no joint bank account and instead shuffled money between personal bank and savings accounts.

Another common see-saw is 'wise' and 'innocent' about money. On the surface, Pete, fifty-two, and Samantha, thirty-nine, should have had similar attitudes to money. They both had childhoods where finances were tight. Pete was the eldest of eight children and his mother struggled on his father's postman's salary. Samantha's father owned a hairdressing salon but was an alcoholic and drank all the profits. So her family had started in a detached house with a garden and ended up in a council flat. However, they drew very different conclusions from their experiences. Pete became money 'wise': reading the financial section of the newspaper, making investments and putting money into a pension fund. Samantha became 'innocent'. 'I know nothing about money,' she joked. 'If an item is reduced by twenty pounds that means I can spend the "saved" money on something else.' The more reckless that Samantha became, the more Pete felt the need to hoard money. 'Sometimes I feel like a little girl, asking Daddy for pocket money,' Samantha complained.

How to defuse arguments about money

The first step is to understand that money means different things to different people. I ask couples to tell each other a story from their childhood. Pete remembered getting a paper round and the extra food it bought. So I asked him what money meant. 'Power,' he answered. Samantha spoke about the pleasure she derived from a shiny new bicycle she got for her tenth birthday and the pain of discovering three weeks later that her father had sold it. So what did money mean to her? 'Enjoy it while you can,' she concluded. Other things money means include: freedom, security, fun, a terrible responsibility, a way of keeping score, a means of corrupting, status, respect. There are as many meanings as there are people.

The next step is to identify your particular see-saw – worried/unconcerned, saver/spender, wise/innocent, hoarder/gambler – and your greatest fear about what would happen if your partner got his or her way. For Carol, the shopper, it was: 'Everything will be grey and dour and have no joy.' Her husband, Jake, was quick to reassure: 'I don't want to stop all your spending.' Jake's greatest fear was that the house would be repossessed. It was Carol's turn to calm him down: 'I'm aware that my wardrobe has got out of hand and I've started selling some excess clothes on eBay.' Ultimately, they were able to see that both ends of the see-saw had value: without Jake's saving, they would be in serious financial hardship; without Carol's ability to enjoy money, there would be no treats and their lives would be very dull.

Another way of understanding your partner's position on the money see-saw is to examine his or her past. Although our take on money might seem fixed, it will often change from relationship to relationship – depending on the other person's personality and attitude to money. When Will, the man who escaped his money worries by fishing and playing computer games, looked back at his first marriage, he had a valuable insight. 'She was entirely reckless and I had to keep a very firm hand,' he remembered. In effect, he had been the 'worrier' in that relationship. He turned to Louise: 'I'm sorry, it must be horrible for you. We should be doing this together.' Ultimately, they had found a middle position where their see-saw could be balanced.

It is only at this point that the traditional solution for money worries – getting out the bills, bank statements and pocket calculator – can come into play. For the first time, Will explained the complexities of his company's sales commissions and why his salary changed each month. Louise felt less in the dark and more reassured. Meanwhile, Carol, the shopper, was able to reveal the extent of her debts to Jake – which turned out to be less than he feared. 'Why didn't you tell me before?' asked Jake. 'I would have felt judged,' explained Carol. When they went through the monthly outgoings in their separate accounts, Jake accepted that the amount he contributed to their joint living expenses was inadequate. (Her debts were partially caused by funding items such as their children's birthday presents out of the supermarket allowance.) They also realised that their accounting system was a hangover from when they first came together and did not reflect the realities of family life. So they opened a joint account.

Ultimately, there is no right or wrong approach to finances. However, dealings need to be transparent and honest and this is only possible if both partners feel that their opinions have been heard and valued first.

ARE YOU FINANCIALLY COMPATIBLE?

Look at the following questions and write down your immediate thoughts on a separate piece of paper. Don't spend too long – your first response is the most revealing. Then give the quiz to your partner to complete and compare results. Discuss the differences and similarities in your attitudes to money, how you could meet in the middle and whether you need to arrange your finances differently.

1. For me, money represents . . . (Write down your top three answers.)

2. Look at the following list and choose your top five spending priorities: car, clothes, home improvements, socialising, eating out, sports/ gym membership, saving/investing, gadgets, holidays, treats, items for the house, children.

3. How much does your partner bring home, after deductions, every month?

4. How much money is it acceptable to spend on items purely for yourself in an average month?

5. What is the biggest amount you would spend on yourself without consulting your partner?

6. Without prior discussion, what is the most you would spend on something for the house or the children?

7. For me, debts are . . . (Write down your feelings/attitude towards debt.)

8. How much debt, excluding mortgage payments, do you reckon that you are carrying as a couple?

9. How much personal debt do you think your partner is carrying?

10. What is your greatest weakness concerning money?

Dealing with Identity Issues

This could be one partner wanting more independence (because they feel smothered or controlled) or someone wondering: 'Who am I?' and 'What do I want out of life?' In many cases, one or both partners are moving from one life stage to another. For example, becoming parents, turning forty, children leaving home or the death of your parents. All of these events naturally make someone take stock and look for something different. Unfortunately, it is easy for this introspection to turn into simmering resentment, emotional exhaustion and a relationship crisis.

If it is your partner who seems, almost overnight, to have turned into a stranger it can be very unsettling. So how should you respond? Ask yourself: Does my partner have a valid point or a reasonable request? Try and separate legitimate desires – like retraining, bettering oneself or trying something new – from what might seem like a personal attack on you.

For example, Patrick felt threatened because his wife, Lucy, wanted to return to college once their two children were old enough to attend school. He put up lots of practical reasons for her staying at home: costs, what if one of the children got sick, and how homework would eat into their couple time. Their arguments soon became about Patrick being controlling or holding Lucy back, rather than the original issue of returning to college. Behind the anger about a partner changing, there is almost always fear. So ask yourself: What am I afraid of? Telling your partner about these fears will probably provide reassurance – rather than another round of argument – and the platform to discuss the changes properly.

How to defuse identity issues

What if it is you who wants to change? Grand gestures, like moving abroad or ending a relationship, often just take the compliant or controlling behaviour to another country or another relationship. Identity is accumulated through small victory after small victory: standing up for yourself, doing something different from what other people expect, understanding your fears and your partner's fears. Here are some pointers on the way:

Look at your internal dialogue: Do you spend more time second-guessing your partner's reaction than examining your own feelings? Do you find yourself trying to 'hold the line', frightened that if you give in over one thing it will have a domino effect and change everything?

Identify which of the unhelpful argument patterns you and your partner fall into: Understanding a behaviour is halfway to changing it. Even if, next time, you find yourself falling into the old patterns, keep one eye on observing yourself. This will make you doubly aware of the pitfalls and less likely to fall into the same traps next time round.

Take responsibility: Don't cast yourself as the victim, look at your contribution to the pattern. As the old saying goes: you can't change anybody but yourself.

Try to understand, instead of trying to convince/ cajole/control each other: Without understanding, it is impossible to build a proper compromise. (For more on this see 'Break out of controlling behaviour' in the next exercise.)

Look at the expectations that underpin your view of the world and yourself: Where does each expectation come from? How much of your identity has come from your parents? How much from your friends? How much from our wider culture, religion, the media? How much of this belongs to you?

Aim for a compromise: Is there a middle way that would balance individual and couple identity?

This process helped Stacey and Carl find a way through Stacey's identity crisis. They had been together since they were eighteen but at twenty-five, Stacey felt, they were like an old married couple. Her internal dialogue was full of questions like: 'Is it OK to want to go out this often?' 'Will Carl be upset with me for wanting to go?' Carl's internal dialogue had gone along similar lines: 'Should I say something about her going out so much?' and 'What will she think about me if I ask her to stay in?' From the beginning of their rela-tionship, Carl and Stacey had both been so keen to please each other that their relationship had been compliance/compliance. More recently, Stacey had run up large credit card bills and Carl had tried to keep spending down: rebellion/control.

Next, 'taking responsibility', Stacey admitted that her shopping had been like that of a reck-less teenager and Carl admitted that he had been like a critical parent; this allowed them to have an adult-to-adult discussion that created a proper budget and put aside money for entertainment. During 'understanding', Carl learned that nights in front of the TV made Stacey feel old before her time; Stacey learned that Carl thought they should be saving to start a family. We had finally reached the unspoken expectations that had been driving them apart. Where had these expectations come from? Carl's parents had had children in their mid-twenties and he said, 'It just feels the right time.' However, Stacey's mother had regretted having children early and had always advised her daughter to 'see something of the world first'.

Finally, the couple were ready for a compromise. Carl started joining Stacey for some of her nights out and saving for a trip to the US. Stacey agreed that she would like to have children before she turned thirty.

Meanwhile Lucy and Patrick, who argued about her plans to return to college, just needed a frank discussion about both of their fears. Lucy was able to reassure Patrick that she was not planning to leave and he was able to be more supportive. Lucy decided to start carving her own individual identity by taking an extra A level part-time at her local Adult Education Institute. 'I wanted to check motherhood had not completely destroyed all my brain cells,' she explained, 'but also to check that I really want this before we splash out a lot of money.' Patrick was happy to babysit on her college nights.

BREAK OUT OF CONTROLLING BEHAVIOUR

The object of this exercise is to understand both your partner's behaviour and your own. Take an issue that causes a lot of tension between the two of you – something that you have argued about frequently in the past or need to argue about!

- The partner who is having an identity crisis or who wants change starts. If this is both of you, flip a coin. He or she talks about how they see the problem, what they want and how they feel. The other person just listens.

- The listener can ask for amplification or clarification but nothing else. No defending, no answering back, no comforting or reassuring. Just listening and understanding.

- If the person who is listening feels tempted to speak, he or she should first ask themselves: Am I trying to convince or to defend? If the

Amy and Harry, in their mid-thirties, had a basically good relationship. They loved each other and their two children, but one stumbling block threatened their relationship: sailing. 'There is nothing that I enjoy more than being at sea,' explained Harry. 'I can forget about my problems at work and just be myself.' Unfortunately, Amy was not a natural-born sailor and didn't want her weekends dominated by a boat: 'The girls aren't that keen either,' she said. Harry quickly countered: 'But they haven't been on a proper trip – just up and down the estuary.' Even the most unlikely dispute would turn into another chance to debate the pros and cons of sailing. So I decided to ban the topic. 'Shouldn't we sort this out first as it's causing us all this trouble?' asked Harry. 'If we can't, I don't think there is any future for us,' added Amy. (This is the sort of hopeless talk that I was seeking to avoid.)

After much discussion, they agreed to concentrate on the other issues between them. I had expected to spend only a couple of weeks improving their argument skills, but I was surprised at how many other problems had been masked by the boat. For example, Harry thought that Amy was too soft on the children and she thought he was too quick to discipline. Other contentious areas included how to spend evenings and their respective in-laws. Previously these differences had fed into their arguments about sailing ('Don't talk to the kids like that, you're not captain of the ship') and the resulting row would quickly become insoluble. With the ban in place, they were able to listen to each other better and make concessions without Harry fearing he'd never be allowed to sail again and Amy worrying about only seeing him if she put up with a cold and wet boat. After a couple of months, they not only became better at resolving everyday disputes but the general tension also reduced significantly. They were ready to tackle their irreconcilable difference.

Instead of allowing Harry and Amy to replay their old arguments – we knew where that would lead – we broke the pattern by doing a brain-storm. I stood by the flip-chart and asked for solutions. Harry suggested buying a half-share with his father in a marina closer to home and thereby cutting down travelling time. Amy wanted to dispute those calculations. However, the rules of a brainstorm prevents immediate evaluation. Every idea, however impractical or off the wall, is written up. Amy suggested waiting until the children were older before buying a boat. Harry wanted to object but I reminded him of the rules and wrote it up. It is important to value every suggestion because it can trigger something better – which it did for Harry and Amy. On the ages of the children, Harry thought they were old enough to crew a boat – as long as it was somewhere calm. Amy suggested the Mediterranean: 'At least it will be warm and, who knows, they might like it.'

Finally, they were able to reach a compromise and agree to a two-part summer holiday with one week hiring a boat and one week on dry land at a resort hotel. Like many couples, when we finally came to the irreconcilable problem, as long as communication had been improved, all the problems had melted away. In fact, for Harry and Amy, the final discussions were almost an anticlimax.

If your irreconcilable differences are caused by infidelity, the communication techniques I've outlined will help you take stock after an affair and negotiate a way forward. However, for more detailed advice, I have written a book on this subject: *How Can I Ever Trust You Again?* (published by Bloomsbury).

Coming Back From a Crisis

Often in an attempt to gain control of an out-of-control situation, the person trying to save a relationship will magnify their weaknesses and promise to change overnight. When Tony told Maria that he had fallen out of love with her, he also confessed that he was unhappy with their sex life. She jumped on this scrap of information, read a million books and promised a better future. Maria was truly in overdrive, overwhelming Tony with love and hoping to win him back. For fear of embarrassing Tony in front of their friends, Maria also kept her problems to herself. Although thoughtful, this decision proved to be counter-productive. Her friends would have stopped her from taking all the blame and humiliating herself into the bargain. Remember the first of my three laws of relationship disputes (see Chapter One): all arguments are 'six of one and half a dozen of the other'. Tony needed to take blame for not speaking up sooner and some responsibility for their inadequate sex life.

So how do you come back from a crisis? Start thinking about the changes that *you* would like. This surprises many clients who would rather keep the spotlight on their partners. Maria was particularly reluctant to talk about her issues: 'If I tell him my problems, he'll think the situation is hopeless. No. I've got to concentrate on the positive.' But this can easily be seen as dismissing the crisis – or, even worse, not really listening. After some prompting, Maria began to think about her needs too. 'Tony keeps himself to himself – I don't know what he's thinking of half the time,' she explained. 'When he doesn't share his feelings with me, I don't really feel like sharing my body with him.' Finally both Maria and Tony had something concrete to improve and their relationship began to turn round. Tony would chat about his day on his return from work, while Maria would try one of the tips from her magazine, for example: keeping good eye contact during their lovemaking (rather than closing her eyes or turning her head away). The following week, Maria and Tony came back with smiles on their faces. He had talked and she had looked, and both felt more intimate than they had for years.

The plan had worked because it had fulfilled three basic requirements:

a) The needs had been expressed as a positive

When you tell your partner (for example) 'You don't talk to me', it doesn't matter how nicely you put it – he or she will hear this as a criticism. The natural response to criticism is either to get defensive or to attack back. However, a positive request such as 'I'd really like to understand more about your job' invites a positive response.

b) They had asked for something concrete

Some requests, even though they are positive, fail because the other partner has no real idea where to start. For example: 'I'd like us to spend more time together' is fine, but how long, how often, and what will the couple do? Contrast this with: 'I'd like us to walk the dog together on Saturday morning.'

c) It had been small and easy to do

Instead of offering something ambitious, like a new position for intercourse or sexy lingerie, Maria had agreed to something she knew would be achievable: keeping her eyes open. Instead of intimate chats about love and where the relationship was going, Tony had agreed to talk about something more neutral: his work.

Whether you are coming back from a crisis or defusing a minor spat, the following exercise is very useful.

THE POWER OF ACKNOWLEDGING

Twenty-five years of couple counselling has shown me that there is nothing more powerful in turning round a difficult situation than the *power of acknowledging*. It not only shows that you are open-hearted, but also helps open up the heart of the other person too. Best of all, it can shift a relationship out of crisis mode and into a phase where both parties can truly listen to each other. So how does it work?

Lizzie, forty-two, has been dating Thomas, forty-five, for twelve months and they came to counselling because they couldn't decide whether to live together or not. Their relationship was complicated because both had children from a previous marriage and Lizzie had a twelve-year-old autistic child. 'He has a mental age of about three or four, which means that he is hard work and I can't give Thomas the attention that he seems to demand. I don't think he understands just how exhausting it is for me, day in, day out. There is no let-up,' Lizzie said. Thomas kept his eyes fixed on the floor and muttered: 'I do know what it's like.' For a while, each partner kept on repeating their basic case – with more and more supporting evidence. Eventually, I threw up my hands: what did they want from each other?

'I just want Lizzie to understand how hard I've tried,' said Thomas. With a little prompting, Lizzie acknowledged that Thomas was patient, kind and supportive and went on to list examples and occasions when she'd been particularly grateful for this. Thomas, in turn, acknowledged how much Lizzie had achieved with her son. Obviously both had known deep down that the other appreciated them, but they needed to hear it! Finally, Lizzie and Thomas were ready to negotiate with open hearts and soon found a formula for living together. Here are the ingredients for acknowledging:

- **It has to be neutral.** Rather than said angrily, sarcastically or with strings attached.
- **It works best with examples.** Instead of just 'Thank you for being helpful' – which is a good start – try something more detailed: 'I really appreciated the way that you rallied round when I lost my passport.'
- **It is often heard loudest when least expected.** For example, on a car trip a couple of weeks later: 'I know that you hate hospitals so it was really nice of you to come and visit my mother with me.' This makes us feel our kindness has not been forgotten and therefore we feel doubly acknowledged.

- **It identifies unspoken feelings.** In difficult situations, communication can be improved by acknowledging the feelings behind the words or the mood. 'I guess you're angry?' or 'Are you sad?' Don't worry if you don't guess correctly, because your partner, friend or colleague will be happy to provide the correct emotion and, instead of lurking unexpressed, all the feelings will have been acknowledged.

Summing Up

With ingrained or difficult problems, a couple can be like two people on a see-saw. The more one partner pushes down on their end, the more the second partner will shoot up in the air. The best way to come closer to each other is to move into the middle. Unfortunately, many people cannot hear the extent or the cause of their partner's unhappiness because they are frightened. However, improving communication can resolve even the toughest problem and save the day.

IN A NUTSHELL:
- Little changes improve the overall atmosphere in a relationship and put down the foundations for big changes.
- By relaxing your stance on a contentious issue, it will allow your partner to relax his or hers.
- Acknowledging the full extent of your problems can be the first step to turning round your relationship.

STEP 7

HOW TO MOVE ON

The goal of good communication is for both parties to express their views, understand each other's feelings, find a solution and finally put the problem to rest. One of the best ways to check the argument has not left a bad taste in the mouth, or provided fuel for future rows, is to look back, re-evaluate and revise.

How to Post-mortem a Painful Argument

Although it is useful to go over the build-up to a row and the issues covered – to identify what helped and what hindered – examining the language used is even more beneficial. Time and again, how a couple argue defines how likely they are to find a resolution and, most importantly, one that sticks. Below is a list of three kinds of language used in an argument. They range from positive at the top, through neutral in the middle and negative at the bottom. During a row, it is likely that you will roam across the full range. What counts is where the majority of your language sits. With mainly negative talk, you are less likely to reach agreement. With mainly positive talk, the chances of avoiding a repeat row or hours of sulking are significantly improved.

Positive

Complimentary: 'That's a good point' or 'I admire your devotion'.

Acknowledging: 'So what you're saying is . . .' or 'I can see that you're angry'.

Agreement: 'You're right about my boss' or 'We both want . . .'

Solution seeking: 'So how do we move forward?' or 'Would it help if . . .?' (This is helpful but be wary of heading here too soon.)

Constructive: 'This is what I would like . . .' (It is important to be up-front and clear about your needs rather than hoping that your partner will guess, or telling him or her what you don't want.)

Neutral

Enquiring: 'What do you think?' or 'Why didn't you phone?'

Checking: 'So what happened was . . .' or 'You're saying . . .'

Explanation: 'My boss gave me a pile of extra work' or 'The bus didn't come'.

Negative

Disagreement: 'I didn't say that . . .' or 'I don't want us to stay late'. (With the second example, we're all entitled to our viewpoint but it is better expressed in a constructive manner: 'I'd like to get home before midnight.')

Excuse: 'We had a rush on at work . . .' (these sentences start like an explanation but change midway) '. . . so I couldn't phone'. (They become an excuse by adding how you chose to react – especially if that choice is presented as inevitable. In most circumstances, we could have found time to call.)

Complaining: 'Don't leave your dirty cup in the sink.' (Still only mildly negative.)

Mind-reading: 'You don't want me to enjoy myself' or 'I knew you wouldn't phone'. (From here onwards, this talk becomes increasingly destructive.)

Dismissive: 'Sure, of course you meant to phone' or 'Don't give me that nonsense'. (This often involves sarcasm, put-downs, sniping, and muttering under the breath.)

Critical: 'You only think about yourself' or 'You're a killjoy'. (Attacking the person, not the behaviour.)

Black and white: 'I shouldn't have to ask for a hug' or 'I'd never do that'. (These are statements which suggest 'I'm right' and 'you're wrong'.)

Self-critical: 'I'm not as good as you at talking' or 'Why would anyone listen to me?'

Hopeless: 'There's no point talking about it' or 'Why do I bother?' (Although some of the preceding language seems more negative, this is the most destructive kind because it closes down the conversation.)

'FLAGGING'

We are not always aware of how our comments are heard. If your partner had parents who put him or her down, they will be conditioned to expect negatives and might, therefore, hear criticism even when none was intended. To get an accurate picture of the impact of your discussion on your partner, try this exercise:

- Make a set of three placards. On the first put a tick (positive), on the second put a cross (negative) and on the last put a dash (neutral).
- Give the cards to your partner and start to explain your case about a reasonably contentious topic. As you talk, your partner listens and (without comment) holds up the relevant card.
- When you get a cross, stop and try to rephrase your comment until you get either a dash or a tick. If you can't translate a cross into something positive, just move on to another point.

- Afterwards conduct a post-mortem. Why did something sound negative and how could it possibly be transformed into a positive? What have you learned about yourself? What have you learned about your partner?
- Change over and let the person flagging have a turn talking.

How to Apologise and be Forgiven

What if your argument has ended in a nasty stand-off? Although it is common to need time to calm down and think through an argument, some couples can be sullen, distant, walking on eggshells and uncommunicative for two or three days. Not only is this extremely unpleasant but it also makes people fearful and likely to avoid future confrontations. My aim in counselling is to cut down the recovery time to a few hours.

So what hinders and what helps? Unhelpful strategies include trying to 'buy off' your partner – for example, offering to make a cup of tea, give a back massage or being extra nice. Your partner will interpret this as not taking his or her feelings seriously. Trying to make a joke out of their mood or the argument will have a similar effect. Hoping for the best or waiting for your partner to soften are also pointless and do nothing to end the stand-off. There are, however, two useful strategies. The first is an invitation to post-mortem the row. If the timing is bad – perhaps you have guests arriving – make an appointment to talk. The second strategy is an apology, but it is more than just saying 'sorry':

- **Acknowledge your part in the stand-off.** For example: I shouldn't have been so critical. (Don't offer an explanation as this could sound like a justification, an excuse or even an invitation for round two.)
- **Hold yourself responsible for the consequences.** For example: I really hurt you.
- **Express sorrow.** For example: I'm ashamed that I opened my mouth without thinking.

This will not only break the deadlock but will also encourage your partner to make a similar apology, provide an opportunity to talk, and promote a better argument next time round.

Back From the Brink

When George, a salesman in his late forties, returned to the family home after having an affair, he and his wife, Cherie, a legal assistant also in her late forties, stayed up late talking for three nights in a row. 'I needed to prove to Cherie that I was serious. Previously, I would have cut the conversation short and worried about being tired for work the next morning,' said George. 'I think she really appreciated that.' 'When George first opened up,' said Cherie, 'I was relieved but it was like a dam breaking, I found myself talking about my dissatisfactions – in particular, how George did not take enough time to woo me before trying to have sex.'

George and Cherie had began to communicate in an open and honest way but these conversations can easily stall, because this kind of levelling with each other can have four accompanying behaviours: blaming, placating, intellectualising, diverting.

Blaming

Definition: To accuse your partner for something that has gone wrong in the relationship rather than looking at your own contribution. Here's an example of this from Cherie: 'You don't give me enough foreplay', and from George: 'You don't pay me enough attention.'

Tackling it: Although both George and Cherie were telling the truth, as each of them perceived it, this cast them both in the role of victim. What would happen if Cherie took some responsibility and rephrased her feelings as: 'I don't ask for enough foreplay' and if George said: 'I don't explain to Cherie what I need from her'? They would both be in charge of their own destiny again. Cherie could show George how she likes to be caressed and George could ask Cherie to switch off the TV when he returned home.

Placating

Definition: To appease your partner with sweet words or offer something to keep them quiet in the short term, rather than address the root problems. George would often reassure Cherie with 'I won't leave you'. Meanwhile, Cherie would immediately give in whenever George complained about something – 'You're right, I've been far too wrapped up in my own stuff' – even if she did not necessarily believe his criticism was justified.

Tackling it: There is nothing wrong with soothing your partner's pain. However, in the long term, constant placating leads to resentment. If George tells Cherie only what she wants to hear, but without really meaning it, he will find it harder and harder to share his true feelings. So what can be done? Placating works well if it is just the first part of a discussion, rather than a stand-alone interaction. Obviously George needs to reassure Cherie he is not about to leave her. However, he must then explain that without fundamental changes he can't stay for ever.

Intellectualising

Definition: Placing an excessive emphasis on rational thoughts, often with a complete disregard to feelings. Here's an example from Cherie: 'Historically, men have always treated women as sexual objects and ignored their needs.' While George would say: 'It makes financial sense to rent a room up in town during the week rather than spending so much on train fares.'

Tackling it: Being rational about a problem can be useful. It helps a couple step back, get a fresh perspective and make the issues seem less personal.

However, a lasting solution has to make sense to the heart as well as to the head. Intellectualising can also get a couple trapped in pointless arguments – about nineteenth-century sexual etiquette – rather than addressing the real issues. So balance the rational thoughts with feelings and the generalisations with the personal impact.

Diverting

Definition: To deflect someone's attention in the hope that they will forget the original complaint. The three main techniques are: denying, distracting or ignoring. For example, George would change the subject from his bedroom prowess by saying: 'Think yourself lucky that I'm not like my boss – he's got two women on the go.' Cherie could try complete denial: 'I'm always interested in what you have to say', when often she would rather watch her soap opera.

Tackling it: Sometimes diverting is an understandable response: especially late at night when one partner feels worn down. However, a more honest approach would be to trade. When George asked, 'Can we talk about this tomorrow?' Cherie was more likely to agree if a specific time and place was suggested: 'Tomorrow, after supper, we'll sit in the kitchen while the kids are watching *The Simpsons*.' Obviously, it is important to honour this commitment. Diverting is only a short-term solution and used indiscriminately will cause long-term problems.

With a little practice, open and honest communication became second nature for George and Cherie. George told Cherie: 'I feel disappointed when you watch TV because I want to share my day with you.' And she told him: 'I feel frustrated when you rush sex because I want our lovemaking to be special.'

Learning

One of the most important elements of looking back, re-evaluating and revising is to identify what you have learned. Anna and Nick, from earlier in the book, decided to stay together. Although the initial honeymoon period was wonderful, both Anna and Nick were worried that they would fall back into their old ways. So I helped them look at why their relationship had developed problems.

'I was always wrapped up with our son,' Anna replied, 'and Nick had his work.' 'When we could have had time together, we surrounded ourselves with friends,' Nick added. 'It was like we were frightened what would happen if it was just the two of us.' 'What were you frightened of?' I asked. 'Arguing,' they said in unison and laughed. 'I didn't want to have terrible rows like my parents,' said Anna. 'My parents never argued, so I suppose I didn't know how to,' said Nick. They had their diagnosis: their love had disappeared because they were never together enough to be intimate and their fear of arguments had trapped them either side of this divide.

Next, I asked them how they had changed. 'We're not afraid to speak our minds,' they answered in unison again. So what could they do if they found themselves heading into trouble again? Nick and Anna didn't answer, they just looked at each other and I knew the counselling was over. By learning what caused their problems – and remembering the new skills that pulled them out – they were confident they could avoid the same traps in the future.

For many couples this is enough knowledge, but others like to look deeper and learn what attracted them to each other in the first place. Everybody's childhood leaves them with relationship dilemmas inherited from watching their parents' marriage. It might be 'not showing feelings', 'coping with unfaithfulness', 'temper tantrums' or 'attitudes to loss' – the list is endless. We are drawn to people who have complementary problems and are wrestling with similar issues. For example, Julia, a thirty-five-year-old secretary, had listened to her mother complain about her father – a travelling salesman – never being around. So Julia, in turn, had no picture of how a husband and wife negotiated daily living together. She swore not to make the same mistakes as her mother, but unwittingly found herself married to a workaholic – who played little part in family life.

Repeating the same mistakes as our parents made might seem depressing but, in fact, we have a chance to re-enact the dilemmas and find a more comfortable compromise. When Julia understood that her anger about her husband's hours in the home office was exacerbated by memories of her parents' fights, she was able to get her reaction back into proportion. She also admitted that she would have hated for her husband to be hanging around all the time, stopping her getting on with her projects. With this understanding Julia and her husband were able to negotiate a routine where Saturday was family time but he was allowed to work on Sunday.

Forming relationships – and having children together – will always rub at the old fault lines from the past and make us question our relationship. While previous generations expected problems, we are more impatient and less willing to tolerate anything less than perfection. However, if we all hung in longer and believed more, we would address the underlying issues and reap the reward of a doubly intimate and doubly satisfying relationship. Here is a final exercise to bring any lingering problems up to the surface to deal with once and for all.

UNPICKING EXPECTATIONS

Below is a list of potential conflicts: write down beside each one what it means to you/what you believe is the approach of a right-thinking person. For example, beside 'debt' you could write: a necessary evil, shame, a personal failure, good money management or a fact of life. Go through them as quickly as possible, so you record your first spontaneous thought. Afterwards, return and ask where these expectations come from: mother, father, friends, media, priest, wider culture, or politicians. How do these expectations feed your arguments? Are any of your expectations out of date? Do you need to change any of them? Which are particularly important to your identity?

> *Sex, money, Sunday morning, debt, television, role of a man in a relationship, role of a woman in a relationship, flowers, being late, paying bills, play, Christmas, credit, experimenting in bed, health, marriage, how time is spent, Saturday night, friends outside the relationship, affection, entertaining at home, the past, communication, hobbies, bringing up children, tidiness, meal times, housekeeping, dress sense, work, alcohol, disciplining children, promptness, birthdays, interest, presents, behaviour around other people at social functions, sport, the bathroom, cuddles, education.*

Summing Up

Discovering why it was necessary to argue, rather than discussing the problem, is an important part of putting things behind you. Simply hoping for the best and trying to appease our partner or holding on to resentment will only store up problems for the future.

IN A NUTSHELL:

- Talking about an argument seldom makes it worse.
- Think about your part in any deadlock, how you could have behaved differently, and offer a heartfelt apology.
- Even the nastiest argument can be transformed into a positive if you learn something important from it.

FINAL NUTSHELLS

1. Taking Stock

The higher the stakes, the more feelings run high, the more crucial the conversation. Unfortunately, these are the very discussions that we are likely to handle badly.

- When partners want different things, they often adopt one of four negative approaches. These include trying to control their partner, rebelling, indifference (persuading oneself something is not important) and compliance (rolling over and letting the other person have their way).
- Although all these approaches work in the short term, they can store up problems for the future.
- There is a positive alternative: cooperation (finding a solution that is acceptable to both partners).

- This goal is helped by adopting three helpful philosophies about relationships: problems are six of one and half a dozen of the other; emotional equals attract, and the eighty/twenty rule (recurring problems are 80 per cent about the past, and 20 per cent about today).

Checkpoint: Start by taking stock of the quality of your comings and goings. What happens when you leave and return home? Do you kiss your partner goodbye or shout as you rush out of the door? When you return, do you talk about your day? How do you greet each other? Are your good intentions derailed by children, preparing a meal, the TV or checking emails? How could you improve?

2. Low-Conflict Relationships

This is where everything is a small problem – so small it doesn't merit discussion.

- Although you seldom fight, there is tension and it feels like you are walking on eggshells or swallowing your discontent.
- Problems rarely get better of their own accord, so hoping for the best is seldom a good strategy.

- With little hope of anything changing, your partner may simply switch off. In the meantime, you imagine everything is fine because your partner has stopped complaining. However, things are only better on the surface.
- Start with small issues and work up to the bigger ones.

Checkpoint: Improve your communication by taking it in turns to talk. Toss a coin and the winner has five minutes to explain all his or her concerns. The other person will listen without interruption and afterwards will summarise what he or she heard – nothing more. No interpreting or giving the other side – just repeating back the main points. Afterwards, swap over – so both of you have a chance to talk for five minutes and to summarise the other's case.

3. High-conflict Relationships

Either both partners' reaction to a problem is to fight – or one fights and the other flees. The first reaction escalates even the smallest issue to something big. The second provides pursuit and withdrawal, or withdrawal with the other partner in hot pursuit.

- Anger is not something that you should express whenever or wherever you want to.
- Having said that, it is not something to suppress either.
- Listen to the message of the anger, understand why you feel so strongly and let it out in a controlled manner rather than a hot blast or an icy withdrawal.
- Make certain that you are angry with the right person to the right degree.
- Be wary of exaggerating your feelings to make a point.
- By allowing yourself to get too angry, you could inadvertently train yourself to get angrier the next time – so that the madder you feel, the madder you get.

Checkpoint: If you are about to let rip, stop and think: will this negative statement only make matters worse? It is always better to praise what was done rather than criticise what was not. With recurring problems, choose a time when you are not angry so that you can discuss the issue and look for a solution – rather than just let off steam.

4. Develop Your Assertiveness

This is when communication is open, because you expect to get a hearing, and honest, because there is no editing of feelings for fear of upsetting anyone.

- Think about what your partner wants.
- How strong are his or her feelings?
- What do you personally hope to gain?
- How strong are your feelings?
- Look at the options and instead of having a winner and loser, attempt to find a solution where both of you are winners.
- Being assertive, rather than aggressive, will encourage your partner to respond in a similar manner.

Checkpoint: Assertiveness training has its roots in the workplace. It is easier to start using the skills in this environment – or when dealing with shop assistants or tradespeople – because the stakes are lower than with our partner. Once you feel confident, you can transfer the skills to the home.

5.   How to Argue Effectively

Arguing is a skill and skills can be taught and, with a little practice, perfected.

- Tackle one subject at a time.
- Bring up issues as soon as possible rather than save up for a deluge.
- Really listen to your partner's case and imagine, if for only five minutes, that he or she is right. After all, this is someone that you love and must, therefore, have some valid points.
- Aim for a compromise.

Checkpoint: Concentrate on your partner's behaviour: 'Please don't leave wet towels on the bed' rather than criticising his or her personality. For example, 'You're slovenly.'

6.   Saving the Situation

With complex and long-running problems, it is helpful to have good arguing skills but even more important to be a good listener.

- Never dismiss a possible solution – even if at first sight it seems ridiculous – because talking it through together will probably suggest a better, more workable solution.
- Although we imagine, for ingrained issues, that nothing we say or do will impact on our partner, this is often because we have tried the same failed strategy again and again or, worse still, in a more and more extreme form.
- Instead of waiting for your partner to change, take the initiative yourself.
- Sometimes, accepting the full horror of your situation, rather than trying to ignore it or play down the severity, and acknowledging the problems ahead, is the first step towards healing.

Checkpoint: When faced with a fresh incident in a long-term problem, the temptation is to react automatically and have some variation of the same old argument. Break out of the rut by doing something completely different. If you rant and rave, try being detached and icy calm. If you walk away, stay and talk. In many cases, the opposite approach can provide a breakthrough.

7. Moving On

It is not always possible to find a solution. Sometimes it is enough to agree to differ. However, it is impossible to move on before:

- Both partners have had a chance to fully express their feelings.
- Both partners feel they have been properly heard.
- All the options have been explored.
- Each partner has challenged their own expectations.
- You have done a post-mortem and learned from any argument.

Checkpoint: Show your internal workings and ask for help from your partner, rather than unilaterally coming up with a solution. If your partner is involved in the decision process, he or she will not only understand but also have a stake in the outcome.

FINAL NUTSHELL:
- Improving your communication is the surest way to improve your relationship.
- Be flexible. Instead of demanding something 'should' happen, ask if it 'could'.
- No subject is too big to resolve if approached in the right way.

A Note on the Author

Andrew G. Marshall is a marital therapist and the author of *I Love You But I'm Not In Love With You: Seven Steps to Saving Your Relationship*, *The Single Trap: The Two-step Guide to Escaping It and Finding Lasting Love* and *How Can I Ever Trust You Again?: Infidelity: From Discovery to Recovery in Seven Steps*. He writes for *The Times*, the *Mail on Sunday*, the *Guardian*, *Psychologies* and women's magazines around the world. His work has been translated into over fifteen languages. Andrew trained with RELATE and has a private practice offering counselling, workshops, training days and inspirational talks.

www.andrewgmarshall.com

THE SEVEN STEPS SERIES

ARE YOU RIGHT FOR ME?
Seven steps to getting clarity and commitment in your relationship
ISBN 9781408802625 · PAPERBACK · £6.99

*

HELP YOUR PARTNER SAY 'YES'
Seven steps to achieving better cooperation and communication
ISBN 9781408802632 · PAPERBACK · £6.99

*

LEARN TO LOVE YOURSELF ENOUGH
Seven steps to improving your self-esteem and your relationships
ISBN 9781408802618 · PAPERBACK · £6.99

*

RESOLVE YOUR DIFFERENCES
Seven steps to coping with conflict in your relationship
ISBN 9781408802595 · PAPERBACK · £6.99

*

BUILD A LIFE-LONG LOVE AFFAIR
Seven steps to revitalising your relationship
ISBN 9781408802557 · PAPERBACK · £6.99

*

HEAL AND MOVE ON
Seven steps to recovering from a break-up
ISBN 9781408802601 · PAPERBACK · £6.99

ORDER YOUR COPY:

BY PHONE: +44 (0)1256 302 699;

BY EMAIL: DIRECT@MACMILLAN.CO.UK

ONLINE: WWW.BLOOMSBURY.COM/BOOKSHOP

WWW.BLOOMSBURY.COM

BLOOMSBURY